OPEN-BOAT CRUISING

OPEN-BOAT CRUISING

Coastal and Inland Waters

Frank and Margaret Dye

Preface by Ian Proctor

David & Charles
Newton Abbot   London   North Pomfret (Vt)

With gratitude to our dinghies and to Ian, their designer. We also remember with warmth the many, many people who have shown us friendship and hospitality in the course of our cruises.

British Library Cataloguing in Publication Data

Dye, Frank
 Open-boat cruising.
 1. Boats and boating
 I. Title II. Dye, Margaret
 797.1'24   GV811.6

 ISBN 0-7153-8247-0

Photoset by
Northern Phototypesetting Co, Bolton
and printed in Great Britain
by Redwood Burn Ltd, Trowbridge, Wilts
for David & Charles (Publishers) Limited
Brunel House, Newton Abbot, Devon

Published in the United States of America
by David & Charles Inc
North Pomfret, Vermont 05053, USA

CONTENTS

PREFACE

Frank and Margaret Dye have vast experience of cruising in dinghies. Most of this has been acquired in their famous 16-foot Wayfarer dinghy *Wanderer*, which proudly took her place in the Greenwich National Maritime Museum after having sailed 40,000 miles with them in 19 years.

Many of their cruises have been epic voyages, mainly on northern waters, from Scotland to Iceland, or the Faeroe Isles, or Norway and above to the Arctic Circle. But there have been many short cruises too, for whenever they have a few spare days, in summer or winter, they try to take their boat to some part of the coast – mostly off their beloved East Anglia, but often elsewhere – to renew their friendship with familiar waters or to explore new areas.

They choose to do their cruising in a centreboard dinghy, rather than a keelboat with a cabin, because they believe it gives them more freedom to go where they want to, when they want to. For instance, they decided at very short notice to sail amongst the Lofoten Isles, in the Arctic Circle thirty miles off Norway, so shipped *Wanderer* out and soon found themselves in magical surroundings of crisp blue mountains, irridescent glaciers and silence so intense they felt they should dare only to talk in whispers – and after the sun had set, turning the fjord aflame with fiery reflection, the short night was almost too warm for sleep. The mobility of a dinghy gave them that experience – how else?

Margaret and Frank keep detailed logs of their cruises – even of their day sails – and these are not merely brusque recordings of bare facts of time, distance, position, course and weather, but they describe places and, above all, feelings. And so, in the many extracts from their logs that are to be found in this book, you can learn not only how to

6

cruise in a dinghy, but the why and the wherefore behind the urge to do so. And maybe while you read you will sniff the sea air and before long be tempted to follow, though perhaps not to the Lofoten Isles – but no need to be so ambitious for there is plenty of beauty, peace and adventure still to be had around our coasts.

Dinghy cruising is not a pastime to leap at without proper preparation and the right sort of boat and equipment. It can be dangerous and the sea is always to be treated with respect. In this book you go along with two friendly experts who, in the extracts from their logs, share their experience and knowledge with you, openly telling you of their joys and fears, comforts and discomforts, and the consequences of their actions, whether good or bad. These pieces from their logs are interspersed with advice from a fund of practical knowledge that only such able and experienced dinghy cruisers could assemble.

Frank and Margaret now have a second Wayfarer dinghy as successor to their original *Wanderer* – also called *Wanderer* of course – in which they cruise together. Margaret also has a 14-footer, as she wanted a smaller, lighter boat which she could sail with a crew, but which she could also manage single-handed. I am privileged to have designed both these boats and when the time came to think of a name for the new 14-foot dinghy class of which Margaret's was the first production boat, it seemed natural to call it the Wanderer Class. I am indeed fortunate to have two such friends sailing in these boats of my design; and those who read this book are fortunate also to be able to share with them their skill and experience – and the happiness they find in their dinghies.

Ian Proctor
Loch Long 1981

1
DINGHY DELIGHTS

Cruising in dinghies is not generally considered a sport for the masses. The average sailing family seems to graduate to a cabin cruiser from the dinghy classes very rapidly, dinghies all too often being considered little more than racing machines, convenient sail trainers or boats for a one-day picnic outing. Yet dinghy cruising is a very old occupation, and few modern sailors can surpass the extraordinary voyages of the small open boats of bygone times. Cobles from Scotland and the north-east of England, curraghs from Western Ireland, kayaks from Greenland, and the Viking long ships – all these variously completed venturesome voyages, travelling far and wide across oceans, without such aids as compasses or charts, let alone twentieth-century ocean-crossing apparatuses. Such voyages amply demonstrate the sea-worthy qualities, stability, and load-carrying capacities of well-designed open boats.

Frank believes that the 16-foot Wayfarer was able to survive the Force 9 seas he met on the way to Norway, half-way across the treacherous North Sea, because the dinghy rose over the waves, bobbing like a cork, whereas a small cabin cruiser, for instance, would have been driven into, and under, the waves. That was admittedly an extreme case but it certainly demonstrates the ability of a man of determination to survive in a very small dinghy. However, there are many advantages of dinghies over keel yachts if one merely wishes to cruise on summer weekends, or on one's annual holiday.

The first advantage is that there is no great outlay of capital. Most open dinghies suitable for cruising cost something between £600 and £2,000, and a handy man, able to do much of the work himself, can pick up good second-hand dinghies for much less. Our first Wayfarer cost Frank £200 in 1957. When she was retired to the National

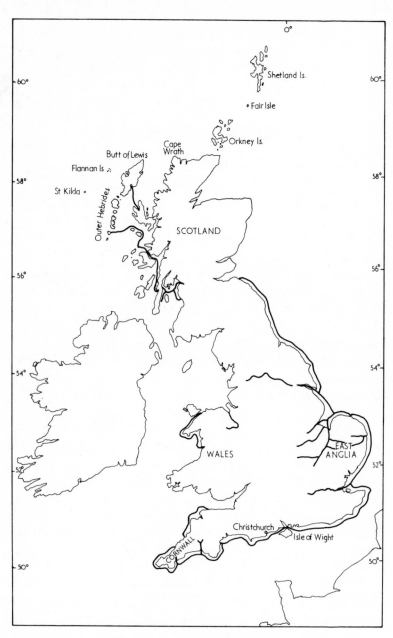

Coastal and inland cruising in the UK

Maritime Museum at Greenwich in 1976, she had carried us about 40,000 miles. We can think of no cheaper, more rewarding, stimulating means of travelling. Our second wooden Wayfarer, bought in 1972, cost four times as much as the first, and we expect her to take us wherever we wish to go for another twenty years. After a house and a car, a boat is possibly a person's third largest capital outlay, but with a cruising dinghy, the capital outlay is such that one need not feel guilty if, for some reason, sailing has to be curtailed for weeks, or even an entire season. Any class of cruising yacht, on the other hand, must mean a capital outlay of many thousands of pounds. Also, by owning a smaller boat, one can afford the best-quality sails, rigging and cruising gear.

Time spent on upkeep is another advantage. Many people get great pleasure from this occupation, and we have several friends who spend more time maintaining their yachts than they do in sailing them. Such occupational therapy – and it is an absorbing hobby, too – is not to be decried, but we like a boat to go sailing in. Our wooden Wayfarer is kept in commission eleven months of the year. (We usually spend February on land.) In mid-July we give her a rub-down, followed by a coat of paint and varnish, before our summer holiday, and she is checked and returned to the water the following Sunday. During the winter all rigging, sails, spars, and the hull are thoroughly inspected which keeps the dinghy off the sailing programme for no more than a week or two. We have friends who laboriously strip out their twenty- or thirty-foot yachts, spending the entire winter working on the boats. But, enjoyable as this can be, they might thus miss a delightful cruise, for the odd out-of-season sail can often be one of the most memorable, as the following log demonstrates.

We rigged our Wayfarer, talking in undertones, and pushed out into the ebb tide. Brancaster Staithe Estuary was peaceful and empty. It was an early December Sunday. As we slid between the empty moorings we gazed delightedly at the unrestricted view of the flat saltings. Normally, in summer weekends, this area undergoes an explosion of yachtsmen. Amid forests of masts, fleets of rubber-suited sailors rush about with trolleys and gear: we have been driven away by such hustle and bustle. But on this day the silence was broken only by the gurgle of the dinghy's wooden hull as she lifted to the swell on the bar. The winds were south-westerly, Force 2 to 3, and the morning felt quite warm. We brewed hot soup on our Optimus petrol stove, swinging gently in its gimballed position beneath the thwarts, and ate our favourite cruising fare – apples, cheese, nuts and dates. As far as the eye could see there was nothing; seawards was a calm, flat, grey, watery waste; landwards, the estuarine beaches glowed a wet gold, as did the stubble fields behind them. Our destination was Sunk Sand. We had our chart of The Wash ready folded, but Frank did not call for it. His experience of sailing these fascinating, shallow waters went back nearly twenty years. I have often watched him scenting out a tide ripping around a sandbank, or sniffing out a watery lead between shifting sands, emerging as the tide dropped. He reminds me of a hunting gun dog, using experience, and senses, to read the signs. And so we sailed on, straining our eyes for the tell-tale wave pattern that would tell us where the sandbank was drying out. We crept along, using the centreboard as an echo-sounder. Anchoring knee-deep in water, we disturbed the fat, cautious seals stretched out on the banks. The recent seal culls had made them suspicious of man, but once in the water they kept close to us, their fat, whiskered faces and black eyes deeply curious. Lumbering about in our heavy oilskins, many layers of woollen clothing and thick Wellington boots, we ran about on the sandbank, some four feet wide and a quarter of a mile long, to restore our circulation. This place was like the very rim of the world, there is no emptier place to visit than The Wash in winter. Deep-draught boats avoid the area, and only centreboard boats, and people with experience find access to this oasis of peace. Sailing back over the bar, the tide bubbled and frothed as it curled over the mussel beds; and it quickly grew dark, so that we had to feel, rather than see our path through the withie way. The grey day slipped into black night, and the gulls fell silent. We washed down the dinghy in a happy silence. It had been a good day, nothing special, just two Norfolk sailors alone in a Norfolk estuary.

Possibly the most easily seen advantage of dinghies over larger boats lies in their summer berthing. Many dinghies are left in club parks all season – waiting lists at dinghy-club compounds are not usually impossibly long – or they are left on village greens or in front gardens. Larger yachts are a much more difficult and expensive problem. Some have wet berths in estuaries, pontoons on riversides, or marina berths, but length for length, the cost of keeping a yacht in a marina, yard, or coastal berth (all difficult to find) is higher than for a dinghy.

The same holds true for winter storage. Dinghies can be trailed home and deposited in the back garden, garage, or slung in the barn roof. Larger boats can also be towed away, but it is not always easy to find fields, garages or spaces close to where one lives, in which to store a boat of over 20 feet. If a boat is stored at a boat yard, the travelling costs, the work, and the rental for the space add up to a great deal over the years.

The annual refit of a well-maintained dinghy need not be a burden, either. Our Wayfarer costs us a few tins of varnish, under-coat, top-coat, and antifouling paint per year, and replacing shackles, rope and other gear is comparatively inexpensive. Several people we know who own larger boats, spend more on paint, varnish and replacements in one winter than it would cost us to replace our entire dinghy.

Crew problems in cruising dinghies are small. Many husband-and-wife teams explore long distances, and the family can also go along. However, Frank, and I, and many people we know, often cruise single-handed, when crew do not turn up. Big-boat owners, on the other hand, are always on the look-out for good crews and compatible sailors to help them sail their boats. Many big-boat skippers we have met sold their boats once their families grew up and moved away, or the wives found other hobbies. We have not met any dinghy cruisers who have had to resort to such drastic measures.

When I have crewed people on bigger boats, there has always been anxiety over whether the crew will actually turn up; then there may be friction, or at best anxiety, until the new crews familiarise themselves with the boat. Often great friends are made this way, and sometimes such settling-in times are relaxing and fun; however, they can be time-consuming. Rigging and getting away for a sail in a dinghy seems a much less complicated and much speedier operation. The skipper can usually do everything himself quite quickly, and a new crew member can come to know the boat while under way.

We made a quick get-away one Christmas. Bidding our guests goodbye after two days of pleasant indulgence, we left the house, littered with presents, thoughtful cards, piles of dirty linen, china and excesses of food, at dawn on a mild, grey Boxing Day, and drove off to get some fresh air. Feeling like inflated Michelin men in all our

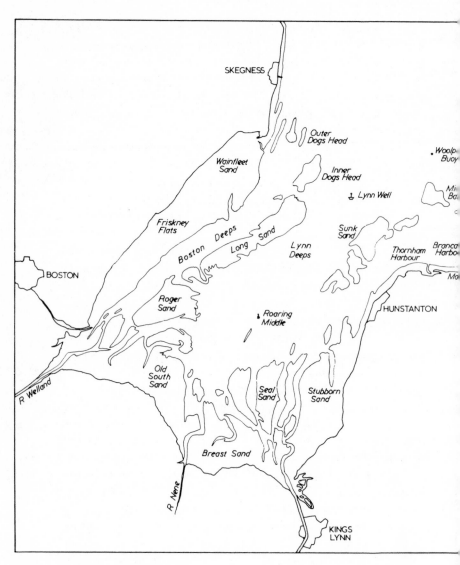

The North Norfolk coast and The Wash, an area of strong tides, shifting sandbanks and bad bars on all the harbours

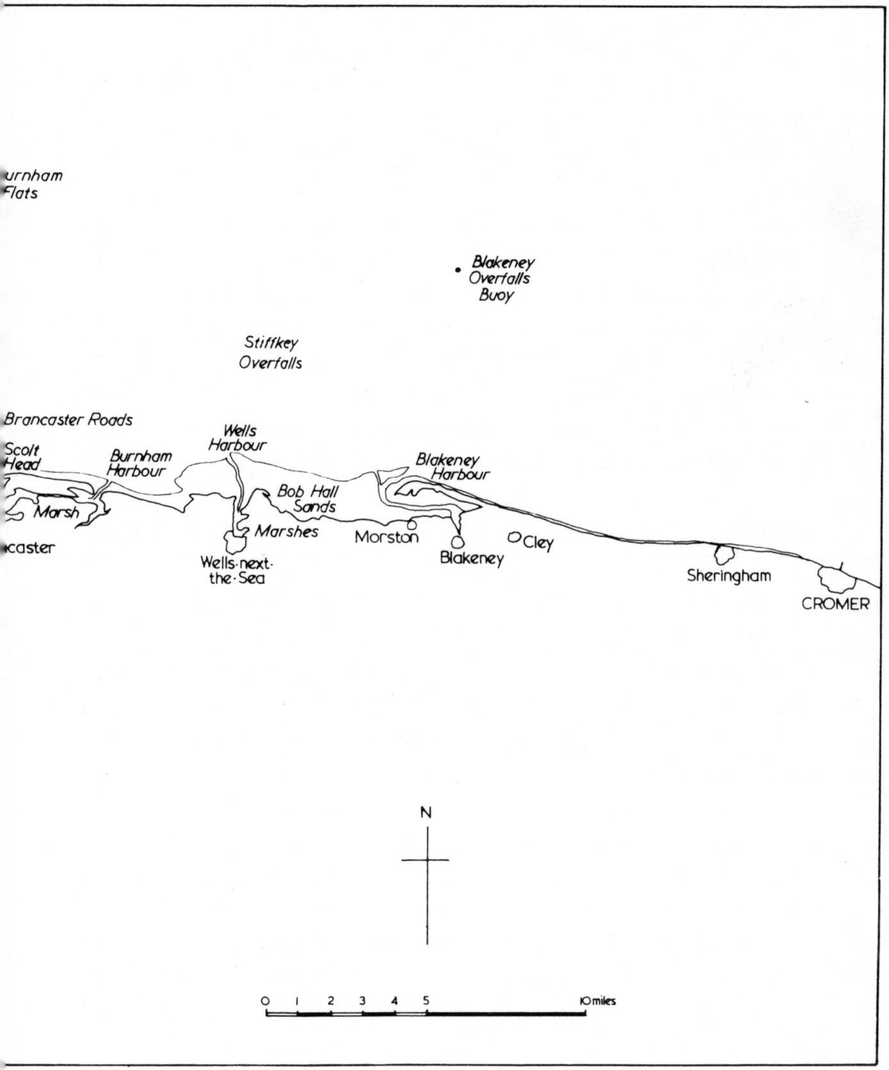

urnham
Flats

Blakeney
Overfalls
Buoy

Stiffkey
Overfalls

Brancaster Roads

Scolt
Head

Burnham
Harbour

Wells
Harbour

Blakeney
Harbour

Bob Hall
Sands

Marsh

Marshes

Morston

Cley

caster

Wells-next-
the-Sea

Blakeney

Sheringham

CROMER

N

O 1 2 3 4 5   10 miles

15

winter sailing gear, we pushed *Wanderer* off the trolley, and, as we sailed over the bar at Burnham Overy, breakfasted on turkey legs and other left-over party fare; then Frank stretched out on the thwarts and slept, while I sailed down the deserted coast, past Holkham woods. The tiller needed only a finger touch, and I have often been colder at sea in mid-summer. All day long we sailed gently along the Norfolk coast – a perfectly relaxed sail after the hectic preparations of business and party life at Christmas time. Willing hands helped us pull the dinghy on to the trolley that night. 'Come and have a cup of tea,' invited a local, as the day light died. So we peeled off our damp layers of sailing clothes, and sat steaming before a marvellous wood fire, and a twinkling Christmas tree. We had just driven the dinghy home, when we heard the weather forecast, which warned of approaching north-easterly gales of Force 8. Next day we awoke to a flurry of snow. Winter sailing can be a great tonic, if one is ready to go when weather and tide are hospitable. I certainly enjoyed that Christmas-present day out.

Often I have crewed several friends on big boats. One year *Twilight*, a Falmouth Quay Punt, took me all round the Greek Ionian islands. It was a great experience, yet I missed the activity and affinity with a dinghy. What hit me very forcibly was the shortness of the season for *Twilight*'s owner, and at least six other owners of larger boats I have talked to. If they were lucky, and early in the queue to get afloat, the yard craned them into the water in early April. What I found so much less acceptable, was that most boats had to be taken out of the water at the convenience of the yard. This could be the end of September or, at the latest, October. What a feast of day-sails can be snatched out of season, by those who are ready and not satisfied with their summer sailing quota.

Our insurance covers us for twelve months of the year, and Frank always remembers a cruise in January after he had trailed the boat to the South Coast before a conference at Bournemouth which had finished on a Saturday morning, so that he had two unexpected free days until work on Monday morning. Depending on the wind, he could sail either westwards to Poole, or eastwards to the Isle of Wight, and then hitch-hike back on the Sunday to collect the car. The weather forecast was for light north-west winds. A powerful torch and chart of the Solent completed his equipment. There was no obvious launching place at Bournemouth, but the commodore of Christchurch Yacht Club readily gave permission to use the club slip. Although most members seemed a little surprised that anybody should want to sail in January, Frank thought he detected a trace of envy as well, for it was a glorious, clear, sharp, sunny morning. Christchurch Harbour is beautiful at this time of the year; there were no other boats in sight, and although Frank was alone, he still had company: a heron flew low overhead; a coot surfaced close under the bows, and looked at him in round-eyed surprise; there were ponies grazing on the rough ground to port. To starboard, in the distance, lay Hengistbury Head, brooding darkly on the skyline. Frank was cutting the corners over the shallows, for it was already one hour after low water, and he was in a hurry to reach the narrow entrance, called the Run, for there would be little chance of beating out once the tide began to flood. He met the oncoming tide fifty yards short of the entrance; it was pouring through the gap like a mill race, but he managed to beat clear by overstanding the entrance on the starboard tack so that *Wanderer* was able to leebow the tide on the port tack until she was almost touching the wall on the north side of the Channel; then, crossing quickly and using the wind eddy round the buildings, he edged along the other bank so as to scrape over the sandbanks into deeper water.

At sea, visibility was much worse than the conditions had indicated – The Needles (which he had come especially to see), the Isle of Wight and Hurst Point were invisible in the blue-grey distance. Having laid off a compass course across the bay at Hurst, Frank sat back to enjoy the sailing, unable to help comparing this area with his native North Norfolk coast. The sea here was blue instead of grey; the sky, even on a winter's day, was also bluer, and freezing as the afternoon was, the air was warmer, lacking the refreshing keenness of an east-coast wind, and Frank missed the wide horizons of East Anglia, and the subtle greys of the North Sea. Hurst Point appeared in due time beyond the bows – a long, low line with a circular fort at the end of the spit, beyond it the dark mass of the Isle of Wight.

The chart gives a useful bearing of Hurst light in line with Fort Victoria on the island, but the visibility was too poor to pick out the Fort against the land mass. Idly Frank wondered why the chart makers had not shown the white stone mansion in Colwell Bay, for it showed up conspicuously and would have given a useful bearing; he commented acidly to himself on their inefficiency – but ten minutes later 'the mansion' had moved along the coast and was now in Totland Bay, and he realised it was the white-painted bridge of a ship stemming the tide down the Channel. He made his apologies to the ghosts of any hydrographers who might have overheard his previous remarks.

There seemed little point in losing time by skirting the Shingles Bank in a boat of only eight-inches draught, for the eddies indicated a reasonable depth of water, but it was exciting sailing as the eddies swung the boat about. Suddenly the temperature plummeted and in an instant it became a cold raw afternoon. Yarmouth, where Frank had planned bed and breakfast, looked unattractive, crowded with idle masts behind the skeleton breakwater, and busy with ferries, so he did not bother to sail closer in to have a look. The next tack took him to Newtown creek – it was much more attractive, but by now he had decided to sail on to Cowes, even though he would not arrive before dark. The sunset was beautiful, the lower clouds hiding the sun and the underside of the upper clouds edged in gold. The island was a dark shadow against the splendour of the evening sky. As the twilight deepened into darkness, the house lights twinkled out from the dark land, and Frank was tempted to pull the boat on to the shore and turn in, but did not have a waterproof cover for his sleeping bag, or a stove.

It is always a good principle to keep in the shallows when there is heavy shipping, and as the light failed Frank began short-tacking close under the land. The little headlands were almost invisible against the dark land and twice he almost ran on to the rocks after having used the torch to look at the chart, thus destroying his night vision for several minutes. There were several fishermen in rowing boats, but Frank sensed their presence rather than saw them. When Cowes Harbour was a mile further along the coast, he watched two hovercraft enter the river at high speed, followed by a cargo ship, and decided that this was no place for a dinghy without lights. Close by he saw a pebble beach in the reflected light of a street lamp, and drove *Wanderer* ashore there. A dog on the promenade panicked as he stepped out of the darkness but recovered his courage somewhat when he discovered that this oilskin-clad figure had a voice. *Wanderer* was soon hauled out on to the pavement by means of a six-part hauling-out tackle attached to a lamp post, and the local police kindly took Frank in their car to the National Sailing Centre where he spent a pleasant evening yarning with Bert Keeble, the Centre's director.

Sunday morning was an idyllic sailing day, the forecast being for light north-east winds, becoming north, Force 4. Bert's wife gave Frank a sumptuous breakfast, during which he heard on the radio a report of an oil spillage from a tanker, with a huge oil slick in Cowes Roads. When *Wanderer* was launched her decks were pure white, a layer of hoar frost covering everything, for it had been one of the coldest nights of the year. The hull soon changed to black as they rolled her down on to the oil-covered beach. By the end of the day's sail, everything was covered in black, foul-smelling oil, but the members of Christchurch Yacht Club readily helped Frank pull *Wanderer* off their ice-lined river and up an icy slipway, and then on to the trailer very smartly. The 200-mile journey back to Norfolk trailing *Wanderer* through freezing fog was pleasant enough, as the car heater was on full blast.

This account gives just one example of the mobility of a dinghy. We have trailed, sailed, and deck-cargoed our dinghy to a different country every summer holiday over the last ten years. At any weekend, we can trail many miles to sail on different waters from our East Anglian base. People who charter share the same mobility, but we have an extra pleasure – we can sail anywhere we choose, in our own boat. We have a friend who owns a beautiful twenty-tonner, based in Poole. Four consecutive summers he attempted to sail to Norway, but each time his holiday dates and the right weather did not coincide. When he finally made landfall in Oslo one summer he had run out of time and was left with only one day to explore, before he had to set off on the return journey to Poole. With our small craft we can explore distant waters without such problems.

One year, for instance, *Wanderer* was locked in during a London dock strike, and so our plans to ship her to Bergen, and then sail on up the coast of Norway towards North Cape, had to be abandoned. Very late in the sailing season, the strike ended, and Frank immediately collected *Wanderer* and trailed her up to the ferry at Newcastle. I was instructed to go with her to Bergen, and then find some means of getting *Wanderer* to the Lofoten Isles. Very much to my surprise this was possible, and I trailed *Wanderer* onto the deck of a coastal steamer, and telephoned Frank that he could join me there. He arrived on a sea-plane as I was watching *Wanderer* being craned into the water from a cargo boat into Lofoten Harbour.

We sailed out of Svolvaer Harbour on a hot, sunny, windless day. The helicopter and seaplane that left shortly after us seemed barely to clear our mast. Our unspoken worries were soon to be answered: how would a dinghy fare so far north of the Arctic Circle? Would the terrifyingly sudden katabatic winds, or the whirlpools dispose of us? How could one anchor in fjords a mile deep?

We spent the first afternoon afloat, dozing and rowing. The blue landscape seemed to stretch into infinity, one mountain range rising into the next, with glaciers, white, tinged with turquoise, falling off the peaks. The silence was impressive. As the light wind fell away entirely at evening, we found a tiny shell beach and a natural harbour behind the offshore islands. Stowing the dinghy, we cooked supper; at midnight it was still light enough to look across to the mainland of Norway thirty miles away. The blue mountain ranges were, according to our chart, 3,000 feet high; the white glaciers looked like icing-sugar decorations. At 0300 hours, the sun had hardly set, and it was too hot to sleep, so we set sail. There was not a breath of wind – we now understood why we had been warned against dinghy cruising in the Arctic, and why the locals relied on motor boats – there was either no wind, or too much. Then, quite suddenly, we were both ensnared by the magic of the Arctic. Its isolation, vastness and silence is something to be experienced, not explained. We rowed on for ten hours, with no wind, and anchored off Tjeldsund. We put up the tent that afternoon in brilliant sunshine, beneath a large ice field. Noses glued to the deck, we watched, as four feet below, on a clear sandy bottom, the marine life poured over the sea bed. Seaweeds of vivid colours and weird shapes streamed in the current, and crabs, shrimps, and fish carried on their lives of love and war, unaware that two human faces were watching them intently. As we arranged our sleeping bags on the floorboards, and blew up our Lilos, we watched the sun set out over the fjord. The calm clear water was ablaze with the reflection. Each time we took a photograph, the next few seconds showed an even more splendid sky. Only the occasional purr of a tiny fishing boat, too far away to be seen, or the slow drone of the coastal ferries, or the soft jingle of sheep's bells on the shore, broke the evening silence. We crept about our 16-foot home, hardly daring to make a noise for fear of dispelling the magical sunset. Finally, the golden ball of the sun rested on the mountain top and then sank behind it. Turning our back on the pink dome, we pulled the tent over the boom and saw the full moon facing us. Yellow, open and unblinking she gazed down on the silent world as she crept over the skyline. In great contentment we heated supper – a tin of meat balls in gravy (utterly foul) and gazed into the silence until we fell asleep.

These adventures, and many others that we have enjoyed with *Wanderer*, all confirm our belief that, with a well-designed and well-maintained dinghy, those willing to learn by their experiences get as much fun and more variety; are less tied to shore-bound facilities; have far less anxiety over berthing and overnight stops; can sail over a much wider area, and pay far less for the privileges of cruising than those who choose larger boats. You might not always be able to boast of long-distance record-beating voyages, of evenings of cabin comforts, entertaining a crowd of friends, and of a dry living accommodation area. And, undeniably, dinghy cruising can be full of hardships, especially if the weather turns bad; and sometimes a gloomy weather forecast might force you reluctantly to drop your cruising plans, but the debit side of cruising in small boats is completely outweighed by its pleasures.

Only recently I had the opportunity to experience both extremes of this sport. I crewed *Twilight*, a 30-foot yawl, around the Greek islands. The deck work was heavy for a small woman, handling the anchor especially, and I found the passages rather boring as there were not enough sailing jobs to keep me busy; then, every evening, there was the panic of motoring around the overcrowded harbours fighting to secure a convenient berth, so as to be able to take on stores, fuel and water. I enjoyed the contrast when I returned to *Wanderbug*, a little 14-foot Wanderer-class dinghy in England and trailed it to Devon, finding nothing but kindness, companionship and offers of help, as I launched and sailed away with pride, skipper of my own little craft, making my own decisions. When I was tired, all I had to do was to pull the dinghy on to a beach and have a rest or go for a walk. Nobody refused to fill my water bottle, or let me shower, or give me a hand up the beach.

At the end of my holiday, I merely tied my dinghy down on the trailer and trailed it home. Once in the garden, it cost me no time or expense, or worries until I was ready to go sailing again. In contrast, the 30-foot yawl in Greece had to be sailed home through appalling weather. To clean and empty the yacht was strenuous and time-consuming work, and after being craned out of the water a month later it stayed ashore for the next five months.

2
CHOICE OF DINGHY

Cruising in a dinghy must be one of the most individualistic of sports, and choice of the boat will be as varied as those who cruise. Dinghies have, however, one common feature – no cabin. At our wedding reception, Frank was sent a telegraph by an earlier crew: 'Now you'll get a boat with a lid on it.' After some years of suffering from slipped discs, I brought up the subject of a more comfortable boat. Frank looked worried, and then designed and had made up a spacious new tent for our dinghy. It provides us with the best of both worlds.

While I had attempted to learn about sailing by the conventional method of crewing on large yachts, getting cold, frightened, seasick, and finding the work very arduous, Frank simply taught himself in a dinghy by trial and error. When the Wayfarer class came on the market in 1957, he had been looking for a suitable cruising dinghy, as he had found his Hornet and other classes of dinghy did not meet his requirements. He employed the engineer's maxim: 'If it looks right, it is right', and bought Wayfarer No 48 without any kind of demonstration or sea trial. He was delighted with *Wanderer*, a boat with no vices, which carried us thousands of miles before we replaced her with an identical wooden Wayfarer.

I wanted to cruise single-handed when Frank was tied up with business, but my weight and size did not allow me complete freedom in the Wayfarer, as I could neither launch nor recover her without help; had to reef, or sail her with small sails in windy conditions, and had to work too hard sitting out to control her properly. I experimented with many smaller dinghies, such as the Leader 14, Enterprise 14, and Luggers, Mirror 10, Gull 11 and Bosun, and got so depressed that I even considered a small dinghy with a lid and keeping her afloat. So I sailed in a Nimrod, and the Silhouette, before

23

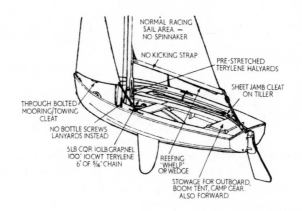

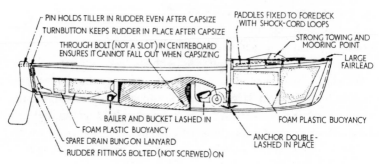

NORMAL RACING
SAIL AREA —
NO SPINNAKER

NO KICKING STRAP

PRE-STRETCHED
TERYLENE HALYARDS

SHEET JAMB CLEAT
ON TILLER

THROUGH BOLTED
MOORING/TOWING
CLEAT

NO BOTTLE SCREWS
LANYARDS INSTEAD

5LB CQR 10LB GRAPNEL
100' 10CWT TERYLENE
6' OF 5/16" CHAIN

REEFING
'WHELP'
OR WEDGE

STOWAGE FOR OUTBOARD,
BOOM TENT, CAMP GEAR.
ALSO FORWARD

PIN HOLDS TILLER IN RUDDER EVEN AFTER CAPSIZE

TURNBUTTON KEEPS RUDDER IN PLACE AFTER CAPSIZE

THROUGH BOLT (NOT A SLOT) IN CENTREBOARD
ENSURES IT CANNOT FALL OUT WHEN CAPSIZING

PADDLES FIXED TO FOREDECK
WITH SHOCK-CORD LOOPS

STRONG TOWING AND
MOORING POINT

LARGE
FAIRLEAD

BAILER AND BUCKET LASHED IN

FOAM PLASTIC BUOYANCY

SPARE DRAIN BUNG ON LANYARD

RUDDER FITTINGS BOLTED (NOT SCREWED) ON

FOAM PLASTIC BUOYANCY

ANCHOR DOUBLE-
LASHED IN PLACE

Some cruising-dinghy features

realising a dinghy was what I wanted. Then Ian Proctor designed a new 14-foot class dinghy, called Wanderer after our own Wayfarer, which came on the market in 1980. She was exactly what I was looking for, and I often go on single-handed cruises with *Wanderbug*. When I crew Frank, however, we always sail our 16-foot Wayfarer.

Generally speaking, any dinghy hull can be cruised with little or no modification. Size is important: anything under eleven feet is too small to sleep in, and too short on the waterline to survive bad seas. Anything over twenty feet is too heavy to have the advantages of cruising dinghies. High-performance dinghies are generally too tender, too wet, lack dry stowage space, and are too light to convert for cruising.

24

The following list covers basic things to look for:

1. LOA. Hull length between fourteen and eighteen feet.
2. Ample beam to give stability. Not too much flare to bows.
3. Wooden centreboard rather than dagger board (wood is easier to repair).
4. Ample freeboard to keep the boat 'dry' in a rough sea.
5. Flat floorboards, so as to enable the crew to sleep and cook and generally operate on a flat, stable, dry platform above the bilges.
6. Good fore and side decks, for sitting and working on.
7. Ample stowage, fore, aft and in the cockpit, with at least one watertight locker.
8. Good buoyancy characteristics.
9. Sound, proven construction, able to resist bad weather and rough handling up and down beaches.
10. Not too heavy in case one wants to drag the boat ashore; or right it after a capsize.

The material of the hull depends on how much time the owner can spare for maintenance, his skill and interest, and his storage facilities. Wooden hulls – whether single or double chine, clinker or carvel built – require time-consuming attention, and frequent painting and varnishing (best done under cover) to keep the weather out, but they will float if capsized or holed, and they have a high aesthetic value. Modifications and attachments are easily made to any wooden boat. GRP (glass-reinforced plastic, ie glass fibre) boats take up less time, a simple washing-off of salt water, polishing, and checking that the gel coat is undamaged being enough to keep it in condition. Dry winter-stowage for GRP is not vital, provided that the hull is drained and satisfactorily tied down.

The conventional rigs have various modifications. A low-ratio rig has obvious advantages if the dinghy is left afloat, or sailed through stormy weather. Many dinghies have masts that are lifted in, and then the shrouds and forestay made fast. If a mast can be raised and lowered in a tabernacle, the boat can slip beneath bridges where much interesting winter- and inland-cruising can be enjoyed. We have had delightful day cruises along the Norfolk Broads, along the Thames, and through many Fenland river and canal stretches.

One of the most interesting of these was a trip we took along the Leeds–Liverpool Canal one autumn when I had a week's half-term holiday. Frank had not been able to get away to cruise all summer, and the tides were unsuitable everywhere in the UK that last week in October, except on the Northumberland and Durham coast, and even here, towards the end of the week, we should be committed to finding our way into unlit, drying harbours on the first of the flood tide at dusk, which Frank considered an unacceptable risk, for although the north east coast is both beautiful and fascinating it is certainly not the coast to take risks like trying to get into small unknown harbours in the dark. The wind had settled into the south-west and had been blowing a continuous half-gale for several days. We were left with a choice of the Upper Thames or the ancient Leeds–Liverpool Canal, if we were not to revisit old cruising waters such as the Fen rivers and the Broads. It seemed worth visiting such an engineering feat as this canal, over 150 years old, and if lucky, we would cross England and get a fair wind into the Humber from where we could sail back to our home port of Brancaster in easy hops. British Waterways told us we could swing *Wanderer* into the water at their Wigan depot, but that we must clear that section of the Canal within a day as it was being drained and closed for winter maintenance work on the locks. I stowed the boat while Frank cleared the paperwork. As he knew the canal authorities disliked sailing boats on canals, he reported that we had a small powered craft (oars!) with a small auxiliary sail area which we might (just possibly) use if there happened to be a 'fair' wind. The shipping forecast was Irish Sea: south-westerlies, Force 8; Humber: south-westerlies, Force 7. The Pennines are approximately half-way between the two sea areas, so for the rest of the cruise we split the difference between the forecasts. It was a good forecast because the Leeds–Liverpool Canal lies roughly north-east from Gargrave before turning to the south-east, and we needed strong winds as the canals are sheltered by belts of trees and industrial areas. We hoisted full sail and cast off, only to realise we did not know which direction to take there being no current, and in the great loop of the canal we had lost our bearings! The next day's sailing was very hard work, as we had to negotiate several large locks, and lower the mast repeatedly to get beneath the bridges, electricity and telephone cables, and the winding gear of a colliery. Along one stretch of the canal, *Wanderer* was sailing to her maximum displacement speed, occasionally lifting on to a plane, and we wondered what we could do if we broached as our sailing waters were less than two boat-lengths wide.

At one point Frank looked over the side of the canal, and suddenly realised that we were sailing above the roof tops, with the streets, factories, and town centre laid out below us. We were crossing the 150-year-old Burnley Embankment, built in the early nineteenth century to carry the canal above the town and across the valley. A day or two later, we found ourselves sailing in a deep cut, then, as we rounded a bend we suddenly came to a hole in the hill – the Foulridge Tunnel. We had seen it on the map without really appreciating its significance – it is a mile long and driven straight through the hill. Here the old bargees sent their horses over the hill whilst they 'legged' their boats through the tunnel. As I suffer from claustrophobia, having once been trapped in a salt cave while touring Austria, I elected to follow the path of the old-time horses. Frank put on my oilskins, lowered the mast in the crutch, got out his torch, and set off through the tunnel. The roof dripped and the darkness became so intense that he had to get out our hurricane lantern. It was quite an eerie passage, and Frank began to wish that he had learnt to scull, but it was now too late to learn, so he had to resort to standing on the foredeck and pushing with an oar against the roof – hard work.

Most dinghy rigs are bermudian or gunter. Older, one-design-class dinghies are still around that demonstrate the versatility of lug sails. If you do not wish to cruise to windward too often, this type of rig, with short spars, is easy to handle and cheap and easy to maintain and repair. The gunter rig is still often seen, but two halyards are usually needed to raise and lower the main, and there is a problem of what to do with the extra spar when camping at night. On the other hand, with the gunter-type rig, you have the advantage of short spars, and performance to windward is pleasing. Most modern dinghies use the bermudian rig. Its windward performance is excellent; when sailing with just the main, or running downwind under jib or genoa, it is safe

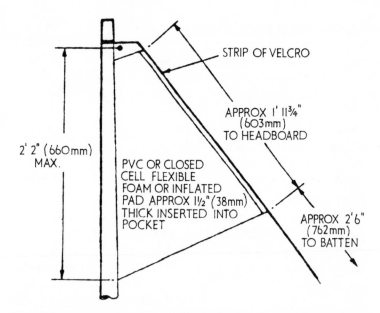

STRIP OF VELCRO

APPROX 1' 11¾"
(603mm)
TO HEADBOARD

2' 2" (660mm)
MAX.

PVC OR CLOSED
CELL FLEXIBLE
FOAM OR INFLATED
PAD APPROX 1½"(38mm)
THICK INSERTED INTO
POCKET

APPROX 2' 6"
(762mm)
TO BATTEN

Mainsail buoyancy pocket: if the dinghy inverts there is a real danger of losing gear; this pocket allows the mast to rest on the water, giving the capsized sailors valuable time to think and sort out the problem

and manoeuvrable; and it is simple to rig and to reef. A few dinghies are two-masted, such as the Salcombe yawl and the Drascombe range. The advantages are that the sail area is spread out and to douse the mizzen means instant reefing; however, working to windward is slower, running is less constant, and they are more expensive to maintain.

Spars can be of wood or alloy. Wooden spars need continual maintenance, unlike alloy ones, and are heavier, but they float, they can be easily modified, and they are easier to repair than alloy spars. On Frank's cruise to Norway he and his crew, Bill, were capsized several times during a severe gale. The mast was tied down in the crutches, and the dinghy lay to a drogue for eighteen hours. After the storm, Frank and Bill still had some two hundred miles to sail to reach Aalesund. With a saw and a knife, they were able to cut away two feet of the shattered mast, lash the remainder with wooden splints and rig a jury mast. It worked, and they reached Norway safely.

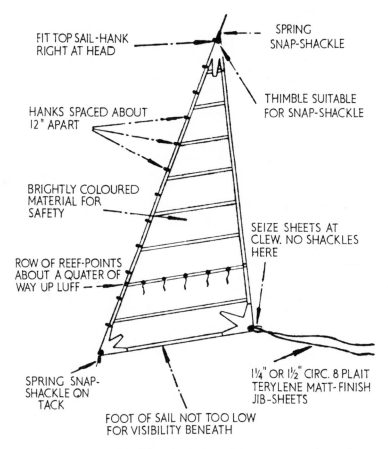

FIT TOP SAIL-HANK
RIGHT AT HEAD

SPRING
SNAP-SHACKLE

THIMBLE SUITABLE
FOR SNAP-SHACKLE

HANKS SPACED ABOUT
12" APART

BRIGHTLY COLOURED
MATERIAL FOR
SAFETY

SEIZE SHEETS AT
CLEW. NO SHACKLES
HERE

ROW OF REEF-POINTS
ABOUT A QUATER OF
WAY UP LUFF —

SPRING SNAP-
SHACKLE ON
TACK

1¼" OR 1½" CIRC. 8 PLAIT
TERYLENE MATT-FINISH
JIB-SHEETS

FOOT OF SAIL NOT TOO LOW
FOR VISIBILITY BENEATH

Cruising jibsail. When single-handed sailing, it is helpful – for ease of identification – to use a long continuous jibsheet, of a different colour and texture to the mainsheet

When cruising, there is not much space for carrying spare or alternative sails. Often one delays changing down until too late, or resists putting up the larger sails because one is too tired to make the extra effort. The most efficient method is to carry full sails that can be reefed quickly and with confidence. Slab or roller reefing is largely a matter of individual choice, and of the size, shape and durability of the gooseneck, and of whether one prefers centre or back main sheeting.

29

Frank prefers roller reefing. He heaves to by backing the jib, removes the lower batten, and then takes as many rolls in the main as conditions demand. This can be done single-handed, and it is an exercise well worth practising. I prefer slab reefing on my 14-foot *Wanderbug* because it can be done more easily, and is kinder on the sails as the shape is not altered, and the kicking strap can be kept in position on the boom. Reefing procedure can be summarised thus:

1. Heave to.
2. Let off kicking strap completely.
3. Haul the leech earing tight and secure.
4. Ease main halyard until the luff reefing cringle is 15–20cm above the boom.
5. Secure the luff earing to luff reefing cringle. Haul tight and secure.
6. Reef, either roll or tie in reefing points along boom.
7. Reset kicking strap (if needed).
8. Set sails and go.

Correct sail balance improves the handling of the boat, increases the speed, and saves unnecessary hard work on the helm. The centre of effort of the sails should be a little behind the centre of lateral resistance of the hull; thus the dinghy will always round up into the wind if the tiller is left alone. Excessive weather helm can be cured either by moving the effective centre of effort forward by 1) using a larger jib, 2) decreasing the mast rake, or by moving the centre of lateral resistance aft by 1) raising the centreboard slightly, 2) moving the crew aft.

The converse applies if the boat suffers from lee helm.

Ideally, the dinghy should be largely controlled by her sails; the rudder merely making fine adjustments. To break a rudder when sailing off shore can be very serious and the following extract of our log of the cruise from North-West Scotland to Shetland demonstrates how necessary it is to be able to sail without a rudder in an emergency, and also to be able to lower the mast whilst at sea.

Just before the 1745-hour shipping forecast, Frank took over the boat, put up more sail and decided to sail for shelter and make landfall on Fair Isle before it got dark. The forecast spoke of gales from the north-west all

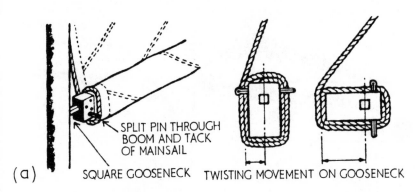

SPLIT PIN THROUGH
BOOM AND TACK
OF MAINSAIL

(a) SQUARE GOOSENECK   TWISTING MOVEMENT ON GOOSENECK

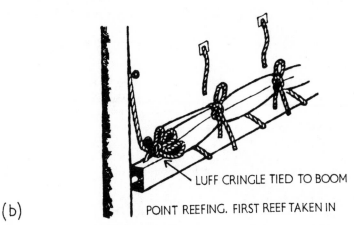

LUFF CRINGLE TIED TO BOOM

(b) POINT REEFING. FIRST REEF TAKEN IN

Reefing: (a) roller reefing; (b) slab reefing. Whichever method is favoured it is important that the cruising skipper can reef at sea, and single-handed if need be

around us, but not in our area. That area has a reputation feared by most experienced seamen. We thought the wind was approaching Force 6. At about 1900 hours, Fair Isle appeared on our bows, looking as though she were being swept rapidly to our port, so fierce were the tides we were sailing through. We were some four miles off, and through the murky light, we could see house lights on Fair Isle. I busied myself with supper preparations; then, over the noisy sea I heard a decisive crack. The boat seemed to go inert, lying helpless in a wave trough. Frank yelled some instruction which was lost in the noise of the wind and waves, but sensing that something had broken, I unfastened an oar which Frank grabbed and pushed through the dinghy's transom slot. With both arms straining, he eventually got the boat under control again, using the oar as

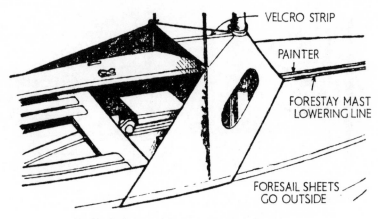

VELCRO STRIP

PAINTER

FORESTAY MAST
LOWERING LINE

FORESAIL SHEETS
GO OUTSIDE

A spray dodger, useful when children are taken along

a makeshift rudder. The stainless-steel spot welding on the pintle had failed. I grabbed the broken rudder and tiller, lashed them beneath the side decks, and continued with the evening meal. All I could manage was a cold sandwich, but it warmed us; we were very cold, having sailed for more than twelve hours under taxing conditions.

An hour later, above the screaming wind, Frank made a decision that sounded as matter-of-fact as asking the time. 'I'm going to lay out a drogue, Marg,' he said. I felt helpless, I had never done this before. The dinghy was bucking like a crazy horse; to stand up would probably mean being thrown out. Somehow, crawling around the dinghy, holding on with one arm, we got a routine worked out. The lashing wind was icy, and the noise was shattering. Frank told me to hold the boom crutches in position on the transom, while he lowered the mast in its tabernacle, using the extended forestay to control its descent. We tied the mast down, tied up the shrouds, laid out the drogue and then lay on the floorboards with the spray dodger pulled over the cockpit area. We felt rather than saw that the dinghy was held head-to-wind by the canvas drogue. It was 2100 hours, the wind was only Force 6, but much of the North Atlantic pours through the gap between the Orkneys and the Shetlands, reversing every six hours, and with a spring tide running into the wind the whole seascape was worse than gale conditions.

Every few minutes the boat seemed to pull tight on its warp, hover, shudder, and then plunge downwards. After a second's halt, the sea would hiss past and the dinghy would lie limp in the foamy waves' wake before gathering to face and climb up another wall of water. We were both very seasick. I knew that Frank was also very angry with himself,

32

because he muttered, 'I am sorry I brought you out here. I always swore that I would try never to be in the wrong place at the wrong time.'

I tried not to think about the dinghy rolling over with us trapped beneath the canvas cover, and I found myself tensing to listen for the next hissing roar of water thundering past, because it meant that the next wave had broken right. Frank listened to the midnight forecast, but as he removed his headphones, I did not ask what it said. I think we both thought that we would be dead by dawn, and there was nothing we could do. 'What's that?' I asked, sitting up from the floorboards. We both strained our ears, because I thought I had heard muttered human voices. We flashed our torches to announce our presence, and then lay down again, almost relieved to be alone; to have been rescued by the Fair Isle boat would have been marvellous, but too disgraceful to endure. Each time I lay down, I heard the undertones of long conversations; each time I sat up to identify the position of the sounds, they disappeared. We were later told that the wooden boat had acted as a sounding board for whales or other sea creatures 'talking' below us.

I thought daylight would never come, and it seemed too cold to sleep, but I must have dozed, because I was woken by Frank saying in quiet excitement, 'Marg, you should take a look at this.' I blinked, expecting to see at least a beautiful sunrise, or a ship close by. Instead, I was horrified to see an endless mass of foam-flecked white water all around and breaking seas dashing at us from all directions. I retreated ostrich-like under the cover again, and marvelled at our dinghy and the effect of the drogue. About mid-morning, the seas seemed less mountainous, and the wind had stopped that dreadful whining sound. Frank thought it had dropped a little. He outlined his plan: it would be slack water in one hour's time, and he thought with the tide flooding with the wind, the seas might die sufficiently for us to sail into the lee of Fair Isle. It was a relief to do something positive. We ate, and then rolled back the cover and raised the mast. Immediately, the boat seemed to roll in an arc of over 40°. We crawled about the boat, working with one hand, holding on with the other one. Once the reefed sail was up, and the oar in position, I was told to haul in the drogue, control the sail with the main sheet and be ready to bale. Frank had both hands on the long steering oar; this was very tiring work because, if a wave hit the hull wrong, Frank had to reverse the oar to avoid a broach. We were fine reaching into very big seas, and the boat was swamped often. If I stopped bailing to be sick, the water rose above the centreboard case; we were knee-deep in water. Slowly we reached the lee of the island and the seas flattened. The wind now only screamed over a bright blue sea. Fair Isle South Harbour was green and peaceful. We grounded, jumped out and pulled *Wanderer* ashore. Looking up through salt-encrusted glasses, we saw about half a dozen men coming down to help us. After a day spent resting and exploring parts of this beautiful, independent island, we thought we would carry on to Shetland. Depressingly, the weather forecasts indicated that the weather would remain very unsettled with a series of lows sweeping in from the north-west.

The islanders told us that we could put *Wanderer* on the decks of their mail boat, the *Good Shepherd*, and warned us of the dangers of 'The Roost', an overfall far more dangerous than the Men-O-Mey in the Pentland Firth, lying between Fair Isle and Shetland. We agreed to travel to Shetland as deck cargo, and then to continue our cruise northwards along the Shetland Islands once the weather had settled. We were very touched when, on arriving at 0600 hours the next morning to load the dinghy on to the *Good Shepherd*, we found every man on the island hovering by to give us a hand. A large yacht had sheltered in the harbour the previous night, and we had watched the crew row to the shops to replenish their stores and row straight back to their boat and disappear. No islander had spoken to them, and we appreciated all the more their kindness to us. As we waited to leave, we talked to the island men, and again thanked the family who had taken our broken rudder from the beach while we slept the previous day. They did not even ask if we would like help mending it: they quietly took it away, repaired it and put back in the dinghy. What a privilege to experience the brotherhood of the sea.

3
DINING IN A DINGHY

Food is such a personal thing that it is impossible to make hard and fast rules. It makes good sense to eat regularly, and to try to have a relaxed and sustaining meal before beginning a cruise (since there may be neither time nor inclination to eat during the first few hours of sailing). Once under way, whether the cruise is a few days' coastal hop, or a cross-Channel or longer passage, a good system is to arrange to eat two good hot meals a day, breakfast and supper, and have cold snacks during the day, which can be eaten with one hand while sailing, or more comfortably off watch. When Frank sailed *Wanderer* to Iceland and Norway, he used this system, whichever man was off watch preparing the dawn and dusk hot meals before taking over the dinghy.

The crew of a small boat with no cabin comforts need food of high calorific value, as it is important to stay warm enough to keep mentally and physically alert, besides which the sheer physical work of a small boat, although enjoyable, can be continuous and strenuous, especially during spells of bad weather, and calories are burnt up quickly. Cold meals and snacks are not necessarily less nutritious than hot meals, but hot food is an instant morale booster. Diarrhoea and constipation are the common unpleasant effects on many people of a break in bodily routine when cruising, and, of course, sometimes seasickness, so food should be chosen taking these possibilities into consideration.

Food usually tastes much better outdoors, anyhow; Frank and I have had the occasional meal at excellent and sophisticated hotels, yet, sitting out in some magical spot simple food, spread out on *Wanderer*'s thwarts, has been even more memorable and satisfying. Frank and I are gourmets at heart, however, and, fanatical cruisers though we are, we do sometimes get bored of our necessarily basic cruising fare; all the more, therefore, do we enjoy the occasional meal ashore. Frank and I had had a hard, wet, punishing sail across the Minch, on our way back from St Kilda. As we rounded up to the harbour wall at Port of Ness, a Scottish lady called down from the pier head to Frank, 'Would your little boy like a cup of tea?' I practically flew up the 15-foot vertical harbour wall, and an hour later we were sitting in a Scottish croft, before a peat fire, eating hot fish pie off Doulton china, which I suspect was only used on high days and holidays.

On another cruise, *Wanderer* was taking us along the coastline of the Norwegian Arctic. The weather had broken and we were cold, wet and tired, and decided it was time to have a break. We tied *Wanderer* to a floating pontoon at Tromso, tidied her up and left her with no worries about vandalism or theft in our absence. A passing taxi showed no surprise when two oilskin-clad figures in large Wellington boots asked to be taken to the best hotel in Tromso. We stepped out of the wet and the cold into the lush carpeted warmth of the Grand Hotel. A relaxing hour-long hot bath gave us enormous appetites and we walked into a beautiful dining room, where we did justice to large helpings of superbly cooked salmon and cod steaks, simmering in shrimp sauce, followed by bowls of cloudberries and cream, listening to a Mozart clarinet concerto, relayed softly throughout the meal.

Sometimes local hospitality can become embarrassing, like the time we cruised to 'the loneliest croft in the British isles', and asked if we might take Jeanie and Laurie, the crofters, for a sail. They gave no formal invitation – they simply laid the table, made up a peat fire, and lit candles. We were expected to stay. We ate, talked, explored and laughed three days away on that lovely island in the Shetlands. On another occasion, Frank landed at Aalesund having cruised from Scotland to Norway, and survived several gales; there he was invited to supper by Mr and Mrs Solbjerg. He expressed an interest in trying whale meat, so the first course was whale meat cooked in a delicious stew. Frank and his crew had capsized 200 miles off shore, and most of their food had been lost, so full justice was done to several helpings. As the dishes were removed, their host said, 'My wife thought you might not like stewed whale, so we bring you roast whale bif.' When this course had been enjoyed the host remarked, 'My wife thought you should try grilled whale bif, in case you did not like roast bif . . .'

One of the pleasures of dinghy cruising is that life afloat can be broken up by meals ashore; this means that there is the privilege of meeting the local people, and making lasting friendships, in a way that those who cruise in big boats cannot so easily do. A dinghy pulled up a beach interests the local people, whereas with a larger boat you generally have to find a harbour, from where you are directed to the commercial eating houses. We remember fresh radishes and lettuce picked for us and brought to our dinghy as we prepared to spend the night on Sanday beach, in the Orkneys, to await a good forecast to sail on to Fair Isle. Another happy memory is of sharing a flask of hot tea, brought along a Danish beach, where we camped en route to Bornholm, by Ken Jensen, a great friend, who reached us just before the customs men came to investigate our reasons for being there. He remarked, 'My wife, Mait, made this tea, because she knows how the English love their early morning tea.' We also remember picking fresh raspberries in the garden of Ian and Betty Proctor when we stopped off, while sailing along the Solent, to thank them for designing *Wanderer*; and Devon cream teas at the home of Jo and Keith Proctor. I also remember fifteen cups of tea and delicious fried dabs aboard a Danish light ship on which we were invited for breakfast, as we sailed past in our passage from Aarhus to Anholt, in the Kattegat. These are only a few of the memories we treasure of people's hospitality during our cruises.

When eating aboard, I feel certain basics are helpful to the beginner cook afloat.

1. Food should be easy to serve, and easy to eat. (I remember once trying to chase slippery spaghetti bolognaise around a plate with a fork, finally drinking it from the side of the plate.)
2. Food should be free from any kind of grease.
3. Food should look attractive, and be presented as attractively as possible. (Frank once gave me green pea soup, and runny

scrambled eggs, all in the same cup, on a night when I was very cold and seasick. When I saw it I was promptly sick again!)

4. Food should be what is liked. It is an effort to eat when cold or feeling queasy, and if you don't like the food the effort is often too much.

5. Plenty of fluid must be consumed. After only five hours without liquid the first symptoms of dehydration begin to show. It is, obviously, particularly important to drink plenty of liquid in a hot climate. While they do not provide the body with much fluid, alcoholic drinks are useful but should be taken with caution while cruising. They provide short-lived heat and energy, and a pleasant feeling of well being, but we only drink alcohol sparingly and only when in harbour, or tucked up in our sleeping bags, knowing we are unlikely to be called out in an emergency. We carry a bottle of whisky aboard, but only to offer to fishermen and other local people we meet. Sometimes, when cruising abroad, it can be the only means of communication.

'Whisky, Whisky,' shouted a non-English-speaking Norwegian shop-keeper, climbing down a rickety ladder from the pier head of a village in North Norway. We had invited him to supper aboard *Wanderer* to thank him for opening his shop especially for us when we needed to buy groceries having completely run out, and then insisting on taking us on a tour of Senja in his car. Hearing his urgent calls, I jumped to our stern locker to take out our whisky bottle, with which we had planned to end the meal, not begin it! He was only calling his dog, which was a Scottish collie.

Cooking aboard, even in ideal sea conditions, is not easy, and a great deal of effort and time can be saved by simply heating up food, rather than going in for proper cooking while afloat. Here, planning can make or mar the enjoyment of a good dinghy cruise; most of the menus should be prepared beforehand. Plenty of convenience foods, whether in tins, packets or plastic tubs, are excellent. Each individual must weigh up whether he prefers heavy tins, or packets of dehydrated food, which are, of course, much lighter but which mean that more water must be carried. In cruising dinghies, weight is a major consideration, and so is the stowage of food; as far as possible, heavy stores should be stowed in the centre of the dinghy.

During coastal cruising, fresh bread, fruit and water can be restocked every few days; OS maps and local guide books, as well as charts, give valuable information about the area to be visited. For more ambitious off-shore cruises, the dinghy may have to be self-sufficient for a considerable length of time. Then, fresh water should be calculated (some liquid is already available in tinned fruits and soups) at about two pints per person per day for all purposes.

How to consume the food is merely a matter of choosing from the large variety of utensils available. We put 'nibbles' and snack foods in plastic containers and shock-cord them in easily accessible places, such as under-deck bags, beneath the side decks, or in buckets by the mast tabernacle. Such foods include cheeses, nuts, chocolates and fudge, dried and fresh fruits, peanut butter and other tinned pastes, and fish and meats, and biscuit-type bread. We use the most basic utensils, perhaps just a plate and a knife. For hot meals, we eat either straight from the billy can, or pour it into insulated bowls or mugs. Metal plates and mugs tend to lose their heat quickly, being good conductors of heat, and can be painfully hot to hold or drink from. China and glass are only for the larger boats. With plates, food can too easily lose its heat, or slide into the bilges. Nowadays, we eat and drink entirely from insulated plastic mugs, which are stored on brass hooks fixed beneath the foredeck. We have different colours for each crew member, and yet different colours to denote which are for savouries, which for sweet foods, and which for drinks. There are some good aluminium cutlery sets which clip together, but they corrode in salt water; and while good stainless steel cutlery is ideal at sea, the cheaper makes can be prone to galvanic corrosion if allowed to come in contact with other metals. Plastic cutlery and serving and cooking utensils are light, non-corrosive, and easy to keep clean.

All foods that need to be kept dry we stow in good-quality water-tight plastic jars and boxes — we find square ones easier to stow than round ones. It is wise to use plastic rather than glass for obvious reasons. Teepol (a detergent good for washing up in salt water), pan scourers, several tin openers, and matches are all put away separately in Tupperware containers, and kept near the food stores.

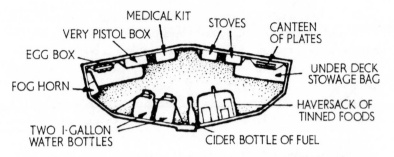

MEDICAL KIT
VERY PISTOL BOX
STOVES
CANTEEN OF PLATES
EGG BOX
UNDER DECK STOWAGE BAG
FOG HORN
HAVERSACK OF TINNED FOODS
TWO 1-GALLON WATER BOTTLES
CIDER BOTTLE OF FUEL

Stowage in a cruising dinghy: it is important to keep all gear weight low down, central and fastened to the boat

Water is best stored in heavy, plastic one-gallon containers. Square ones take up less space than round ones. A good screw top with a small opening solves the problem of spillage and salt-water contamination. It is more convenient to use several smaller containers rather than fewer larger containers as they are easier to refill and carry, and, in the event of a capsize, some may stay with the boat. They should always be shock-corded to the boat.

In large yachts, many people hate their turn to go below to prepare a meal for the boat crew as they may get seasick. In a dinghy, there is not this problem, as everything is done in the open air. And there are usually fewer utensils to wash up. However, to cook in a dinghy can cause many cramped caterers to long for a larger boat with warm cosy galley and running hot water, so life must be made easier for the cook in an open dinghy. A gimballed stove, with a wind shield round it, a place to put a hot billy can or saucepan, and a stable platform to prepare and serve the meal are necessary basics. We never light the stove in heavy weather, and rely on cold food, or vacuum-flasked food and liquids, prepared earlier. On an easy reach or run, or in calm conditions, however, we brew up and cook in relative ease on the dinghy floorboards. We usually heave-to if we want to cook on passage. Too many saucepans, kettles and bowls can make meal preparation a strenuous misery to a tired crew. Stackable utensils that can be easily reached, identified, carried and stowed away are part of the satisfaction of choosing the cooking gear. Small pressure cookers have many advantages. Stoves are largely a matter of personal preference: the basic choice is between those that run on gas, methylated spirits, petrol or paraffin (kerosene). When I cruised in Georgian Bay in Lake Huron, Canada, and barbecued on Antipaxos, and other Ionian Greek islands, there was no tide, and so the dinghies could be left at anchor while we searched for driftwood, and enjoyed cooking over an open fire. Walking back and forth to collect dinghy items was no problem, since the water level hardly varied. Cruising where there are strong tides means that to stop, cook and eat on shore has to be fitted into the tidal pattern and water-level variations.

For cooking afloat, bottled gas (such as Gaz, which I use when cruising single-handed in *Wanderbug*) is clean, instantly lit and available everywhere, but a spare container should be carried. Two-burner stoves are a luxury; usually a one-burner stove is sufficient for simple meals for two people. Gas cylinders and their gas rings can be stowed beneath the side benches, or in the lockers. When full the larger containers might affect the distribution of weight in a dinghy, but smaller gas cylinders are more expensive to run, refill, and you have to carry more spares. Alternatively you can use stoves that run on solid fuel, which are cheap and safe. Liquid fuel is also extremely economical; it is easy to obtain almost anywhere, and easy to check the consumption against stock. The Optimus range of stoves are small and extremely efficient. They can be used with either petrol or paraffin. The Primus stove, which consumes paraffin (kerosene), is also a robust, serviceable cooker, provided you remember to carry spare prickers and primer. In the Wayfarer Frank and I use an Optimus petrol stove, being extremely careful using petrol in a boat, and Frank welded gimbals on the stainless-steel oven. The small stove, with inbuilt pricker, slips into the base of the oven, into which can fit two billy cans on a lower (boiling) and a higher (simmering) shelf. We keep it on its gimbals beneath the centre thwart, on the windward side of the boat.

The Wayfarer Association held a small-boat-cruising Winter Weekend at Cowes National Sailing Centre one January. Various types of stoves were put near a wind machine, on a tilting movable base, and a pint of water was boiled and timed. Valuable evidence was thus collected: the small, wide-based Primus and Optimus stoves

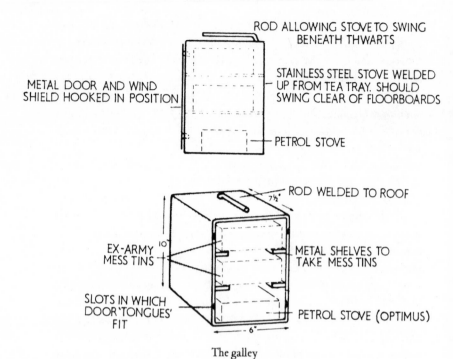

ROD ALLOWING STOVE TO SWING BENEATH THWARTS

STAINLESS STEEL STOVE WELDED UP FROM TEA TRAY. SHOULD SWING CLEAR OF FLOORBOARDS

METAL DOOR AND WIND SHIELD HOOKED IN POSITION

PETROL STOVE

ROD WELDED TO ROOF

EX-ARMY MESS TINS

METAL SHELVES TO TAKE MESS TINS

SLOTS IN WHICH DOOR 'TONGUES' FIT

PETROL STOVE (OPTIMUS)

The galley

boiled water quickly, and proved stable platforms for their size, and were generally seen to be the most efficient types.

Another Wayfarer meeting was held at Crab Searle's Sailing School at Emsworth one weekend. Various members demonstrated how and where they stowed their cruising gear. By trial and error, every individual had found their own solutions. Generally, everybody agreed that heavy food stores should not be packed at either end of the dinghy, otherwise the pendulum effect would cause the dinghy to pitch and become excessively wet; also the sailing performance is grossly interfered with. In *Wanderer*, we stow all tinned food amidships, but not near any compass. The tinned food is colour-coded by paint, stacked in rucksacks, and shock-corded beneath the centre thwarts, on either side of the centreboard. Fresh fruit and milk, and light items, wrapped in plastic bags, are stowed in square buckets or bowls with secure lids and packed either side of the mast tabernacle. This leaves either end of the boat for the stowage of the lighter gear, such as sails, tent, spare clothes and small books and charts.

Fire is a great danger and when cooking in a small dinghy, chemical or powder fire extinguishers must be carried. Asbestos mats are simple to pack and are also useful for simmering and as table mats: hot dishes and pans spoil varnish and plastic surfaces only too easily. An asbestos blanket is invaluable — it can be thrown over flames or wrapped around an injured person; it can be used to nestle food containers in so that they retain their warmth or continue stewing; you can even steam rice, for instance, this way.

When it comes to eating, dinghy cruisers have a reputation for 'pigging it' — which may certainly be true of Frank and myself — but on a Welsh Wayfarer rally in the Menai Straits area I decided that we ought to improve our culinary standards, and suggested that the evening menu should be the subject of our rally competition. The sailing was interesting, and the return sail delayed because we all got stones jammed in our centreboards whilst rolling ashore for the midday picnic. That evening, busy erecting night tents, and generally organising the camp site on Abermenai beach, I thought the long day's sail would mean that our people would rather just put their tents up and sleep than cook an elaborate meal. So I went to sleep, unaware that Hazel Grainger was preparing pineapple, ham and shrimp cocktails, and fresh fruit flan, which Peter, her skipper husband was not allowed to eat, as it was laid out tastefully on the dinghy decks to await the expected menu competition inspection. Another menu offered rabbit cooked in wine in a pressure cooker, and yet another of Norfolk dumplings. I am ashamed to this day that I slept soundly on instead of judging that competition!

4
CLOTHING

The choice of clothes worn in a dinghy can make all the difference between a comfortable and an uncomfortable cruise, so I should like now to discuss the factors influencing this choice. One general point is that the effects of salt water and sun ruin good clothes, so we always sail in our oldest clothes.

When cruising in fine weather sunburn is a great danger since it is so easy to rush unprepared into the sun, laze in the dinghy and the following day suffer the unpleasant consequences of this sudden exposure. Clothing in these circumstances should consist of protective loose shirts and trousers until the skin is sufficiently used to heat, sun-glare and the reflected light from the water. Good sunglasses, sun-barrier skin creams and hats should also be brought along.

The British climate makes consideration of foul-weather gear an unfortunate necessity. However hot it appears when launching, it is always far cooler out on the water. It is generally believed that clothing makes a person warm, but proper clothing merely reduces heat lost from the body to the atmosphere. Any significant change in the normal body temperature of about 37°C can cause, at the least, discomfort, and often rapid deterioration of efficiency (in such cases the dangers to the body can be insidious, because heat loss is often not recognized, appreciated, or dealt with quickly enough). It is alarming to consider that in temperatures of 5°C a man of average build would be hypothermic (ie below viable body temperature) and helpless in less than half an hour if he fell overboard. Probably many people who were assumed dead through drowning in the *Lakonia* disaster actually died from hypothermia in waters of about 18°C.

Oilskins are the most vital part of any foul-weather cruising gear and sailing movements should be carefully made to avoid tearing them. A hole in them in warm weather may be merely uncomfortable but on a serious dinghy cruise exposure could result. Oilskins, made of oiled seal-skin, were used by the early Vikings, but there are now many varieties of waterproofed material including woven nylon, plastic-impregnated nylon with taped seams, plastic terylene and PVC with welded seams. One-piece or two-piece suits are individual choices. We prefer high-waisted trousers and sailing jackets, rather than smocks, as these are easier to get into. Over-generous-sized waterproof clothing is practical because it is easier to move about in, more easily removed, less constricting when more under-clothing is needed and you can retire into it, whelk-like, on those cold night watches when the extremities need protecting. If the waterproofs are too tight they will not be comfortable or practical on a cruise of more than a few hours. Hoods attached to the smocks or jackets are a great comfort but separate sou'westers are more adaptable, and allow one to hear more clearly and move more easily. Wet suits, although a great boon to the racing man, are not a good idea if cruising for considerable periods as the skin cannot breathe, they cause skin chafe and are virtually impossible to get in and out of in a small dinghy. Since the best ones are most efficient when immersed, they have little importance to a cruising man, who sensibly avoids capsizing his well-laden dinghy-home!

The main thing to remember when selecting clothes to wear beneath waterproofs is that body moisture and condensation must be absorbed somewhere and that still air is a poor conductor of heat, whilst moving air greatly facilitates the escape of heat from the body. Thus the most effective under-clothes are those which absorb moisture and trap pockets of still air next to the body. Woven materials are good in this respect, since they can breathe − so avoiding an unpleasant build-up of condensation and moisture − and at the same time discourage excessive air movement.

My first long-distance cruise with Frank (Hebrides−St Kilda) can be taken as representative of our standard practice; Frank literally had to pull me into my clothes, which consisted of the following: long-sleeved woollen vest, long woollen pants, flannelette pyjamas, string vest, 'Old Harry' shirt, corduroy trousers (two sizes too large), two large woollen jumpers, a canvas smock, one-piece oilskins with inbuilt buoyancy, neck towel, woollen gloves with long cuffs, fleecy balaclava helmet, large waterproof PVC gloves and Wellington boots outside three pairs of long woollen socks. No wonder we were described as 'Michelin men' and that the effort of 'spending a penny' was prodigious! We normally carry a spare set of similar clothes, double-wrapped separately in plastic bags which are then loaded into a large plastic bag and stowed in the stern locker. Shore-going clothes consist of walking clothes, plimsoles and acceptable day clothes so that we will look inconspicuous if we become town tourists.

Good sleeping equipment, in which you can sleep warmly and deeply, also goes a long way to making a cruise enjoyable and successful. There are many types of sleeping bags, and you largely get what you pay for. Good-quality down sleeping bags are expensive but warm and light and easy to stow; unfortunately they do not take kindly to salt water. Such bags should not be washed, and dry cleaning is not recommended by many manufacturers. In contrast, artificial-fibre sleeping bags are more bulky, much less warm but salt water is no problem as they wash well. They are also cheaper. We often use a down sleeping bag inside an outer terylene one. A partly inflated Lilo, Karrimat, plastic padding or waterproof bag is ideal to protect the sleeping bag, keep you off the cold floorboards, and also to provide some form of padded insulation. Some dinghies lend themselves to bunk beds, whilst in others it is preferable to sleep on the flat floorboards, keeping the weight low in the boat. All sleeping gear should be well aired when weather permits, and kept in tightly sealed containers or plastic bags, and stowed in the driest part of the boat. It is always easier to stay warm and dry, rather than to get warm and dry again after a wetting.

Safety at sea cannot be too highly stressed. Lifejackets are better than buoyancy aids for serious dinghy cruising. They should be of approved Department of Trade design, and ready for immediate use. Inexperienced crew and children should wear them at all times. On our cruising dinghy, Frank thinks lifelines are even more vital for each crew member than lifejackets. Expensive harnesses can be bought at any good chandlers; some have whistles and flashing lights incorporated. Frank makes ours out of pre-stretched terylene line, with a breaking strain of one ton. The bowline attaches high on the chest and over the shoulder, with a snap shackle; the other end is tied around the dinghy thwart. Its length is twice the length of the dinghy, ensuring that the crew would float clear of the capsized boat, or be towed face above water.

To emphasise the importance of lifelines, Frank's extract from his St Kilda log explains how I nearly drowned when I fell, unconscious from seasickness, out of our dinghy when helming in a vicious Minch cross-sea. We were deep reefed, and he was working out the navigation.

> I look behind, and find Marg gone backwards, unconscious, with her feet still jammed beneath the straps. I grab her lifeline, and try to lift her aboard. I shout to her, but no sign of life – eyes wide and staring – horrible. *Wanderer* gybes heavily and I almost get her inert, heavy, waterlogged body aboard, but the boat heels over dangerously and I cannot get sufficient purchase. The rush of water turns her sideways, putting her back at an even more unnatural angle – Oh Christ! Head goes under water; I begin to panic. I manage to get a grip on myself, and begin to think. I must remove her feet from the toe straps, tip her overboard, then recover her head-first. Unfortunately her built-in buoyancy is not inflated. A brutal remedy but the only possibility as she is unconscious and cannot help herself.

On several occasions, Frank and I have been accused of looking like 'floating Army and Navy Stores', so one day I decided to improve the image of the dinghy cruiser. I was helped by our good sailing friend, Tony Newman, to organize a Wayfarer weekend rally at the same time as the Aldeburgh Festival in Suffolk. I have memories of that rally which I shall never forget. Piers and Greta Ploughman, in their Wayfarer *Sea Urchin*, travelled from the Orwell estuary and met the rest of us launching in the Alde estuary. The flood tide took us up the estuary to the internationally famous Snape Hall, where we all heard Montiverdi's *Vespers*, impeccably attired in evening dress and suits. After the concert, we returned to our dinghies, replaced concert clothes in their plastic bags, donned our cruising clothes, and took the ebb tide downstream to camp in a dream spot on the beautiful estuary. That is a nice way of hearing music!

On another occasion, after several days hard sailing to windward, I had only energies left to keep warm and dry, and able to take my watches. We landed at Yarmouth, after a sail along the east coast. I was cold and seasick. Bending over the mooring lines, I heard my husband give an appreciative wolf-whistle. Looking through salt-encrusted glasses, I saw an elegant blonde attired in a pink silk shirt and white skin-tight trousers. 'How lucky you are to be taken sailing,' she told me. 'I get left ashore to mind the dogs whilst my husband is away sailing Dragons.' I leapt ashore, showered and polished, and half an hour later felt the proudest wife alive, eager to be back at sea, and completely forgetful of discomforts. Without that timely dig, I should have not made the effort, and forgotten how important such morale boosters are to both skipper and crew.

Saturday night at Brancaster Staithe, Norfolk, waiting to catch the early-morning tide. This is our Mark II tent which allows sitting headroom throughout the tent; it is thus really spacious compared to the Mark I ridge tent

Shooting a bridge on the Macclesfield Canal, near Frank's hire-fleet basin. The technique of lowering mast and sails is being demonstrated to Wayfarer Association members on a Winter Weekend (*Stuart Swindon*)

(*Above left*) Mud is always deceptively dangerous: a long oar prevented Margaret from sinking in this south-coast harbour. It is essential, if caught, to keep moving, keep one's steps small and not to panic or struggle

(*Above right*) Yet another use for a long oar: as a substitute for a broken rudder

(*Below left*) Frank navigating in the open dinghy, 200 miles inside the Arctic Circle

(*Below right*) The crew, attached to lifelines, waits for a breakfast of green-pea soup and six-egg omelette – all in one mug! The oven can be seen swinging beneath the thwarts

5
WEATHER SENSE

Successful dinghy cruising depends on your ability to judge the weather. To be caught in an unexpected gale in a large yacht can mean little more than an uncomfortable ride, whereas the same weather could prove disastrous for a dinghy. It is one thing to set out when a gale is expected – something no experienced sailor would contemplate in a small boat – but quite another thing to survive bad weather if caught out on passage. Such experiences turn sailors into seamen.

Everybody setting out of harbour should get the shipping forecast for that area, and also a local forecast. These you can hear on the radio: the shipping forecasts are broadcast at given hours daily, and gale warnings are broadcast before them. Local radio stations also provide local weather and gale warnings. The television weather charts and forecasts are excellent. We always telephone the local meteorological office before setting out, and we have found many RAF stations are extremely helpful and chatty.

The sea takes time to build up – about three hours – and a cautious cruising man plans his coastal hops within this limit so that he can land on a beach or enter a harbour before conditions become dangerous. Weather forecasts are more accurate than is widely believed and their inaccuracies are usually in timing, rather than in wind force and direction. They can, of course, be wrong but they do give a general picture of what the weather is going to do. An experienced sailor will watch the weather pattern for several days before his projected cruise, so as to get an impression of where the areas of high and low pressure are sitting, and how fast they are moving.

In addition to professional forecasts, most yachtsmen should learn to predict the weather themselves. They can do this by watching the cloud formation and direction of movement, and by listening to the

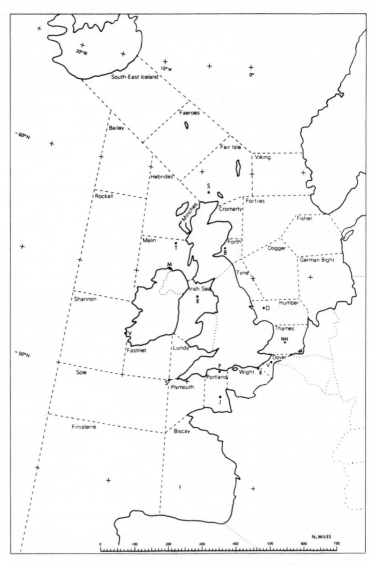

Sea areas of the British Isles, used in weather forecasting

wind strengths and learning to estimate them, and being aware of possible switches. A third aid to self-help weather analysis is by watching the barometer, which some dinghies carry.

The decision to set off may be a hard one – but it is often harder to decide not to go. Once committed, the die is cast, and one just gets on with the job in hand – which is usually to make a safe landfall – without causing hindrance or annoyance to anybody else.

If you set out with alternative plans for good and bad weather, or a variety of places to turn to should the weather suddenly change, it is surprising how often good passages can be made. A snatched passage is often as safe as any calculated risk can be, and the satisfaction, in retrospect, is enormous. A case in point is a cruise we went on in Norway one summer. Frank had planned it over a year before, but as usual we could not plan the weather! There had been a succession of gales – all forecast – and we had not sailed for three days. We were getting very frustrated, seeing our holiday slipping away, while we walked around harbours and anchorages in North Norway, and eventually we set out between gales when a few hours' calm could be expected before the next low came in.

We had a spectacular sail up the Grotsund Fjord, running before the rolling waves, heads hunched deep in balaclava helmets, and feeling insignificant beneath the massive scenery. The near-gale brought a long fetch because the Grotsund Fjord is open to the sea, but all went well. Next morning the forecasts at 0600 and 0700 hours spoke of *kuling* (gales). However, as there was only a moderate south-westerly blowing we decided to sail until the gale came. The mountain peaks above the glaciers looked as though the trolls had sprinkled them with icing sugar. We had been told that dinghy sailing in the Arctic was not easy and that there was either too little wind or too much, but on that day we had half-a-day's glorious sail before the next gale broke.

An inexperienced sailor will more readily sail on a marginal forecast than one who has learned sea sense. It takes courage not to go, particularly if you have driven a long way, or promised a crew a sail. Sometimes the weather can look appalling, but if the forecast seems to indicate that it will not deteriorate further, it pays to rig and

BEAUFORT SCALE OF WIND FORCE

Beaufort Number	Description	Speed in Knots*	Speed in mph*	Height of Sea in Feet (Metres)†	Probable Max Height of Sea in Feet (Metres)†	Deep-Sea Criteria
0	Calm	Less than 1	Less than 1	—	—	Sea mirror-smooth.
1	Light air	1–3	1–3	$\frac{1}{2}$(0.15)		Small wavelets like scales, no crests.
2	Light breeze	4–6	4–7	$\frac{1}{2}$(0.15)	1 (0.3)	Small wavelets, still short but more pronounced. Crests glassy and do not break.
3	Gentle breeze	7–10	10–12	2 (0.60)	3 (1)	Large wavelets. Crests begin to break. Foam is glassy.
4	Moderate breeze	11–16	13–18	$3\frac{1}{2}$(1)	5 (1.5)	Small waves becoming longer; more frequent white horses.
5	Fresh breeze	17–21	19–24	6 (1.8)	9 (2.5)	Moderate waves, and longer; many white horses.
6	Strong breeze	22–27	25–31	$9\frac{1}{2}$(3)	$13\frac{1}{2}$(4)	Large waves begin to form; white crests more extensive.
7	Near gale	28–33	32–38	$13\frac{1}{2}$(4)	20 (6)	Sea heaps up; white foam blown in streaks.
8	Gale	34–40	39–46	18 (5.5)	25 (7.5)	Moderately high waves of greater length; crests begin to form spin-drift. Foam blown in well-marked streaks.
9	Strong gale	41–47	47–54	23 (7)	31 (9.75)	High waves; dense streaks of foam. Crests begin to roll over.
10	Storm	48–55	55–63	29 (9)	40 (12.5)	Very high waves with long overhanging crests. Surface of sea becomes white with great patches of foam. Visibility affected.
11	Violent storm	56–63	64–73	37 (11.3)	52 (16)	Exceptionally high waves. Sea completely covered with foam.
12	Hurricane	64+	74+	44 (13.7)	—	The air is filled with spray and visibility seriously affected.

* Measured at height of 33 feet above sea level.
† In the open sea remote from land; in many tidal waters wave heights – especially their steepness – are liable to increase quickly with a change in tidal direction.

go out to 'have a look'. Often it looks worse than it really is. What should really make the decision about whether to turn back or go on is the calculated risk that a safe landfall can be made.

One June day in 1980 we took part in a Wayfarer rally, with everybody meeting at Orford to launch at 0500 hours. Tony Newman, the local organiser, and an experienced cruising sailor, rang the RAF local meteorological office at 0430 hours, before we set off. The rally consisted of three Wayfarers, one Wanderer dinghy and one Miracle dinghy. His account of it illustrates how decisions about group cruising take into consideration timing, distance to be travelled, knowing what weather to expect, and the predicted conditions and sea state for the end of the passage.

East Coast Rally 14–15 June 1980 I will divide the account into three parts since there were three crucial decisions that were made:
1. *0515 at Orford Quay* Wind N/NE 3–4, overcast, some rain. I had spoken to the local RAF met office at 0445 and they had forecast N/NE 3–4 and then becoming S 5–7 with the passing of a front and subsequent clearance. They timed the clearance and increasing wind for midday or soon after, but predicted a smooth passage of the front up until then. With this slightly dubious forecast I decided we should go down to the Alde entrance and see what state it was in and leave the decision as to whether to go down the coast until then.
2. *0630 at the Alde Entrance* Wind N 3–4, overcast, some rain. All the boats grouped together and I metaphorically put my toe in to see what it was like. The conditions were as expected – a little chop on the bar but the sea relatively quiet and the wind steady and as forecast. Included in the decision to go were a number of factors. The tide had just started to flood down the coast, the wind was fair and with the tide, so with the benefit of wind and tide I estimated about a $\frac{3}{4}$-hour passage down to the Deben. The Alde and Deben entrances both have shoals running NW–SE on their north sides, so at low water are protected from the sea, which was another important factor. The shipping forecast was unpromising but told us what we knew already – N 3–4 becoming S 6–8. I estimated at worst we had five hours in hand. On this information I decided to go.
3. *0700 3 miles south of Orford Haven* Wind N 5–6 increasing. Once we had left Orford Haven we all sailed quickly down the coast in fairly close company, but inevitably the fleet became somewhat scattered – always a problem on any rally. Piers and Greta Plowman took up the

'tail-end-Charlie' position in their Wayfarer and I led, sailing with Margaret Dye in her *Wanderbug*.

At first it wasn't obvious that the conditions were deteriorating, as is often the case with a following wind. I think one tries to pretend that it isn't getting worse, but it was happening fairly quickly and soon the waves were undeniably bigger and cresting a lot more often, and the boat was becoming less manageable. I became apprehensive, looking back at the Miracle. I then saw Piers and Greta round up behind us in their Wayfarer, *Sea Urchin*, and sail over towards them; they were some 200 yards behind by now. The two other Wayfarers were slightly ahead – one well to each side. I think I suspected that the Miracle had a problem, but *Wanderbug* was now a handful and my attention was elsewhere. When I next looked back the gap between us had widened considerably; the wind was still increasing and reefing became imperative. This took a while and by the time we were sailing again the two boats behind were barely visible, in the conditions, and the two boats in front, who hadn't stopped to reef, appeared to be sailing past the Deben Entrance. Both Margaret and I realised that the position was far from happy, but the only thing I can recall saying was, 'I wish to hell we were the only boat out here.' Heartfelt, but not very helpful. There were two possibilities:

1. To beat back into a very nasty sea against the tide to see if the others were OK, or

2. To go on into the Deben and show the other two Wayfarers the way in, which is far from obvious to newcomers at low tide – particularly approaching from the north.

I decided to go on into Deben for several reasons:

1. We probably had one actual casualty at the moment, but 4 more potential ones in the deteriorating conditions, spread over a mile or more of coast – a nightmare position.

2. I wasn't sure that *Wanderbug* would make any headway into that wind and tide with the state the sea was in.

3. I didn't think we could do anything more for the Miracle than Piers and Greta were already doing – not realising that Piers no longer had a rudder.

4. I knew Felixstowe Ferry and thought we could get assistance and effect a rescue more successfully than with the craft presently available – namely ourselves.

This sounds clear and calculated – it certainly wasn't at the time; it was no more than a jumble of thoughts, but I think these were the factors that persuaded me to go on into the ferry.

We turned the buoy at the Deben Bar which was, as anticipated, relatively quiet, given the conditions of a north wind and the low tide, and happily the two Wayfarers, now more than $\frac{3}{4}$ mile beyond, saw us and followed us in.

As soon as we were in the lee of the entrance, we beached and I went down to the ferry jetty where to my great relief I found Charlie Brinkley, the ferryman. Very quickly we were steaming back out over the bar in *Late Times*, his ferryboat, stopping only to collect my binoculars from *Wanderbug*. Charlie immediately contacted the coastguard on VHF, and explained the situation as far as we knew it. Just as we were crossing the bar a red flare went up to seaward. It was impossible to work out who had put it up since there were three boats unaccounted for. We had met Howard Darby coming in in his Wayfarer as we steamed out, but Bill Padgham was not to be seen, nor were Piers and Greta and the Miracle. The binoculars were useless with the spray and rain. We then spotted Bill Padgham's Wayfarer ashore by a groin in the lee of the bar, safe and sound.

Once at sea we saw Doug Goodall in his yellow fishing boat alongside the upturned Miracle. By the time we arrived, the crew, looking like drowned rats, were aboard and bound for the ferry. All the time Charlie was on the radio co-ordinating the rescue with the coastguard and a helicopter which had arrived on the scene from another job further out to sea. The helicopter went up the coast and reported Piers and Greta at anchor and OK. We left the Miracle and steamed up to them some $\frac{3}{4}$ mile northwards – a slow process in the conditions.

The scene, when we drew level with them was unforgettable: the sea was a turmoil, there was lightning, with thunder and rain, not to mention the wind, Force 8 now, Charlie reckoned, and in the middle of it all, this serene, tranquil pair, smiling. As they came aboard Piers said simply, still smiling, 'Don't worry, worse things happen on land!'

We join Piers Plowman's story as the fleet sails down the coast: 'The other Wayfarers and the Wanderer made good speed down the coast. The Miracle, though going well, could not keep up with them, so we sailed back and forth to keep an eye on them. In retrospect, clearly, the weather rapidly worsened so that *Sea Urchin*'s management took a significant amount of our attention. As ever we were late reefing, and I suddenly noticed that the Miracle had swamped. I shouted across to them to stuff a sweater in the centreboard slot before attempting to bale. Then we sheered away from them to roll in plenty of reefs. We did this (uncomfortably) and on the way back I noticed an odd feel to the tiller. Two minutes later our entire rudder blade parted from us and floated away. Very well, we can steer, after a fashion, with an oar, which we proceeded to attempt to do. But in those mounting seas, reefed and with a rescue on our hands, we just could not manage her.

'By now we were coming down to the breaking seas on the bar. While we had been preoccupied with our own boat the Miracle had apparently capsized several times and was now riding upside down with a broken centre plate. We just couldn't get over to her — some two or three hundred yards away. So we downed sail and I got the oars out – but no progress whatsoever; I dipped them in, pulled like mad, and where they next went in was where I had just pulled them out. Greta came to help but with no rudder steering was impossible.

'They had been in the water now for all of half an hour, and we were no closer though we could hear their cries for help. There were no other boats visible, the rest of the fleet had (rightly) run for shelter. So we cast anchor, desperately hoping that at the full length of our warp we could somehow steer across to intercept them. We did all we could, but they passed us with a thirty-yard gap; the warp I threw fell short and they were gone. No more messing; out with the flares – first a yellow smoke, then a red hand-held, and almost at once a fisherman in a stout inshore boat came bearing up towards us. I shouted across the message and pointed downwind and straightaway he steered off to effect the rescue. At the same time an RAF Rescue helicopter appeared and kept watch over the scene. When the youngsters were safely in the fishing boat, the helicopter sailed up to us, but we felt reasonably safe bobbing at anchor so we gave them the OK sign and they went on.

'Immediately, another boat appeared, not a fishing boat, but the Felixstowe ferryboat. As well as the ferryman, there was Tony Newman – much delight. With a struggle we weighed anchor – brutal wind and tide. Having secured a heavy warp to the thwart, and led out through the transom, *Sea Urchin* was ignominiously towed in, stern first. We were all in the ferryboat by now, and apparently this is the only safe way to tow an empty dinghy in a seaway: towed from the bows she is likely to sheer about and capsize.

'At last we were in, with a pretty rough day's sail behind us. There were other Wayfarer sailors arriving, all looking cheerful and anticipatory. We asked them the time – it was only 08 30 in the morning.'

Conclusions I think everybody involved learned a lot from the incident; some of the conclusions are obvious but are no less important for that.

1. *Weather Forecasts and Local Conditions* We were unfortunate that we were caught out in the first of a series of thundery squalls that lasted on and off for the next ten days. It was not forecast even three hours before it arrived and I think yachtsmen must expect to be 'caught out' once in a while. It was a fairly short-lived squall – the wind was down to 4–5 two hours later, before it went into the south and increased again in the afternoon, as the forecast had predicted. The forecasted 'blow' was a

much more serious affair, which underlines three points:

(a) An up-to-date forecast is essential – they are right 80 per cent of the time, and the local ones more often than that.

(b) Getting 'caught out' is an occupational hazard that has to be allowed for by having the right equipment on board and by knowing what to do as the wind gets up, particularly being able to reef.

(c) Knowing something about local conditions – tides, bars, etc. It is always worth having a chat with somebody who knows a particular stretch of water. Remember there are Wayfarer sailors the length and breadth of the country who are only too willing to pass on information; the Wayfarer Log Library too is packed with local information. (The log library and the slide collection are maintained by Wayfarer cruising enthusiasts and can be hired by members of the association.)

2. *Boats* I am saying nothing new when I say that Wayfarers (and Wanderers) are very seaworthy boats and no one will be surprised to hear that they coped excellently in the conditions – even in the hands of relatively inexperienced crews. The Miracle did not, though the crew did everything in their power to rectify the situation. It points to the obvious general conclusion that the boat must be suited to the task it is being asked to do, and to the more specific conclusion that a fleet is only as strong as its weakest boat (crew).

3. *Fragmentation and Rescue* A fleet of dinghies gives a false sense of security on the 'safety in numbers' principle. This is a misconception, except under limited conditions. Once conditions get difficult, each crew has his hands full coping with his own dinghy, and this is his priority. A cruising fleet always fragments to some extent; under difficult conditions this happens even more – as some reef earlier than others, and so on. This can be seen from the earlier accounts. Obviously if a dinghy is in trouble, another will try to help, but it is very difficult indeed. All they can do is to attempt to get another crew out of the water; not only is this also very difficult, but there is the problem of overloading the rescuer. I think that all one can reasonably expect is for another dinghy to go and raise the alarm. This is a depressing but, I think, realistic conclusion, which leads to the next point.

4. *Equipment* Each boat, when it goes cruising, must be a completely self-contained entity, with all the necessary equipment to cope with conditions or situations it is likely to meet, which means compass, charts, flares, anchor, warp, etc. Whilst the Miracle had all these, they were lost during the capsizes, and if Piers hadn't had them, I suspect things might have gone differently. So not only are they absolutely essential, they need to be of good quality, and well secured to the boat. And this I think applies even to very modest cruising.

5. *Reefing* Deciding to reef is difficult and people always seem to put it off – perhaps because when reefing becomes necessary the boat is a handful and reefing is another problem to cope with – not logical, but understandable. In the event, only Piers and ourselves reefed – and both of us long after we should have done. The others didn't and got away with it, but it would have been much safer to reef. I think the best way round the problem is to practise it on the water until it becomes an easy operation, and the crew knows exactly what to do, which will make it quicker and easier when it has to be done in danger.

6. *Hypothermia* The Miracle's crew were all suffering from this when they came ashore – one fairly seriously. They had been in the water just over $\frac{1}{2}$ hour or so, and this points to a very real danger. On the same morning a Wayfarer helmsman at the Aldeburgh Open Meeting was pulled from the water after $\frac{3}{4}$ hour, barely conscious, suffering from hypothermia. There is no space here to go into any detail, but anybody who goes sailing in a dinghy should be able to recognise the symptoms, and learn how to lessen the dangers if they are in the water some time – and indeed how to treat hypothermia. It is very simple and written up in many publications.

There are many other lessons that we learned from the experience but I think these are the important ones.

The most dangerous of weather conditions for sailors is fog. A dinghy can creep along in the shallows and at least avoid shipping lanes and the danger of collision, but it is probably better to get ashore, or anchor until visibility improves. On one cruise neither of these alternatives was practicable. We had left Mousehole in Cornwall, with a good forecast. The morning was sunny and the wind filling in as we left the charming little harbour on our route around Land's End to St Ives. A mile or two out of harbour, we heard the murmur of a fishing boat, but on looking round could see nothing. Suddenly, out of the mist the boat bore down on us: only then did we realise how quickly the mist was closing in; a thick white damp fog suddenly descended. The coastline was blotted out and the wind dropped to nothing. Frank had chosen the strongest tides of the year to sweep us round the coast, and even with the sails hanging limply, the tide rushed us along. Visibility was possibly less than 100 yards. 'The tide will keep us clear of the rocks,' said Frank cheerfully, as he prepared to row. Mile after mile I steered, peering into a white cotton-wool world. Occasionally, I would yell out that we were approaching rocks. The water seemed to boil around them, and I shuddered to think what would happen should we be swept over one and holed. The coastline, which was invisible, was anyway quite unclimbable. After six hours of favourable tide, it suddenly changed and we found ourselves being rapidly swept backwards. Frank thought we could land at Sennen Cove. As we approached where we thought it should be, we heard the boom of the surf; and that with no wind. I did not think we could haul the laden dinghy up the beach. The sunlight broke through the fog mid-afternoon and we crept close to the shore, but could see no suitable place to pull out and wait for the fair tide, so Frank finally decided to anchor and wait overnight for daylight. He tied all the available anchor warps together and hoped that the anchor had taken hold. We were in deep water. That was the longest night of my life. 'We've done all we can, Marg,' said Frank, and he turned over on the floorboards and slept. Having a vivid imagination, I kept sitting up, seeing the sheer cliffs looming and fading and imagining them coming closer. The mournful moan of the fog horns and Bishop's Rock lighthouse boomed out all night.

Eventually Frank, awake again, decided that the tide had turned in our favour, and we rowed on. 'One must trust the compass,' said Frank. Knowing that the coast lost in thick fog was on our immediate right, I was still convinced that I saw looming shadows of cliffs all around us: fog plays most peculiar tricks on all one's senses. When we landed on the beach at St Ives later that morning, I stretched out in the sun to dry out and sleep. A man came up to look at the boat. 'What is your boat?' he asked. 'A Wayfarer,' I answered sleepily. 'Didn't some fool sail one of those to Iceland?' he said. I'd heard that remark before, so I kept my eyes closed until our visitor departed.

6
HEAVY WEATHER: ST KILDA

Our cruise to St Kilda illustrates how a dinghy can cope with a great deal of really bad weather. Having decided to sail there, we spent the winter planning. Frank ordered the charts of the Hebridean area, and studied the pilot guides, while I wrote to the National Trust, Ministry of Defence and other authorities that had anything to do with St Kilda. Over the months, I got letters of disapproval, and others of downright condemnation. It was generally agreed that only the professionals sailed to St Kilda, and that amateur seamen in a small, open dinghy should not consider such a passage. I burnt those letters in case we should not return and they were proved right; instead I read all I could about the area.

The St Kilda islands are the remotest in Great Britain lying 110 miles off the mainland of Scotland, and 45 miles west of the Outer Hebrides. They have the highest sheer sea-cliffs and the tallest stacks of Britain. The island group, comprising St Kilda (Hirta), Soay (Norse for sheep island), Boreray (Norse for North Island) and Dun, form a perfect sanctuary for wild life in the North Atlantic, and thousands of gannets, fulmars and puffins breed there, as also do rare mammals – notably the Soay sheep, and the St Kilda field mouse and house mouse – and the St Kilda wren. Hirta, on which there is a village, is the main island. Village Bay, guarded by Dun, a craggy breakwater nearly 500 feet high, is the only safe landing and that only to be approached if the wind is not from the south-east. Most of the stacks and smaller islands of Soay and Boreray present too steep rock faces where landing would be virtually impossible.

In late July we trailed to Skye and launched. We sailed, uneventfully, to Pabbay, where while waiting for a good forecast, we rested, cooked and walked over this lovely uninhabited island. We

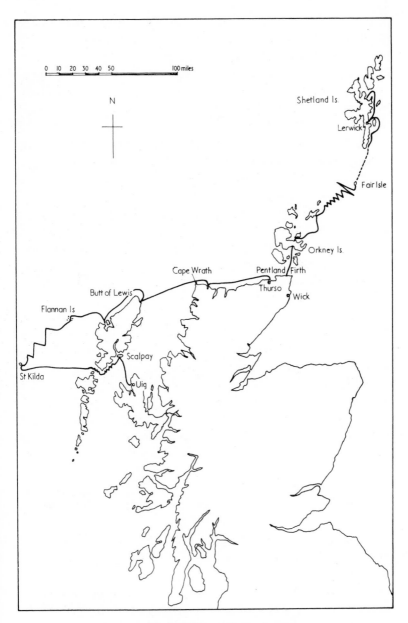

Routes of the St Kilda and Shetland voyages

were both nervous and yet looking forward to making a landfall on St
Kilda, forty miles away. At 2130 hours, with reefed main and small
jib, we pulled in anchor and set out on the longest leg of our journey.
Course 290°, wind northerly, Force 4. We agreed an estimated speed
of three knots, and Frank told me to take the first watch of two hours,
while he tidied up the dinghy. I had never sailed at night before and
when he lay down on his Lilo and slept, I felt very lonely and exposed
to my inexperience. At about 2300 hours I called him to help me reef.
It was a pitch-black night, blowing hard from the north, with a heavy
swell running and occasionally breaking over the boat. Frank rolled
down the main to the second batten and then prepared a tin of self-
heating cocoa. I thought I would never sleep with the incredible noise
of the sea beating on the wooden hull, but the next thing I knew, I
was back on duty. The night seemed even darker and there was
nothing to guide me except the flap of the sails, but suddenly as I
steered into the claustrophobic darkness, I saw a star directly on the
bows, low down on the horizon. In my relief to have a guide I steered
towards it, never taking my eyes off it. We were sailing fast, even
with a deep reef, and big black waves seemed endlessly to pour down
beside the boat. Suddenly, there was a deafening crack, the boat
seemed to go mad, a huge wall of water seemed to curl over the boat
and fall into it, bursts of phosphorescence darting all over the sky. I
was totally disoriented and felt the tiller go limp and unresponsive.
Frank came up and swore loudly, and began to pump out the boat. He
soon discovered that I had done an uncontrolled gybe in following
'the star': the classic beginner's mistake! It was the mast-head light of
a passing trawler! Once the boat was pumped dry, we got back on
course. Heavy squalls from the north were still overpowering us, and
Frank reefed to 18 inches below the hound band, then went back to
sleep.

At dawn – about 0330 hours – I nearly awoke Frank in my
excitement; I had got a glimpse of land – it had to be St Kilda. At
0530 hours Frank saw it too, dead on our bows about twelve miles
distant. There was an isolated rock to the south of the main island,
and Boreray was upwind of the main group and to our starboard. At
0600 hours Frank shook out one reef, at 0610 hours the second. By

shipping forecast times, at 0645 hours there was so little wind we barely had steerage way; however, the forecast told us to expect a north to north-westerly wind, Force 4–5. Frank had estimated our arrival to be by 0900 hours, but at 1000 hours we were sitting becalmed about five miles off St Kilda, and at about 1115 hours I was cutting a sandwich lunch, watching a calm sea, while Frank was studying the charts, with a limp tiller in his hand. Then out of nowhere came an enormous squall from the west. A sudden sheet of rain deluged the area, driving almost horizontally. *Wanderer*'s gunwale was under water and we were almost capsized although not moving. Frank let the main free and jumped up to sit out the boat, while I jumped for the windward side of the dinghy; and, with water pouring in, we were driven sideways, half the dinghy under water. Since we had no steerage way when the squall hit us, the tiller did not answer and the boat could not be luffed. The sudden, violent, silent squall left us, and the boat came upright half full of water. Both of us shaking with the shock and with relief that we hadn't capsized, we pumped the dinghy dry and began another slow tack towards the islands. Before the squall we had been close-hauled within one mile of the main island; the squall had driven us sideways, and when the rain lifted, we saw that we were two miles to leeward of the same headland. We tacked slowly across the mile-wide Village Bay and towards the spectacular island. Peering around excitedly, we didn't see a sign of life. About midway, we closed the stone jetty and two soldiers appeared and waved us to tie up behind their dory, calling out, 'Come in, No 5, your time is up!' Securing the dinghy, we put out fenders and sat back to absorb a view as majestic and overpowering as one could expect to see. The whole island seemed to slope in a hollow bowl towards us like an amphitheatre; and at the bottom was a slight plain in which was situated the old village. Strung out parallel to the water's edge, rising to a grassy slope trailing upwards, was the central peak of the island. We saw dozens of small stone buildings about fifty yards apart, dotted all over the slopes. These were the dry-stone-walled cleits built by the St Kildans to store and keep dry their food supplies. The Army's radar scanner was visible on the ridge at our top left-hand side, the beach and slipway were straight ahead, and the army huts clustered on the shore to the right of the bay, while, towering majestically over the sites of man were the land masses. A few people collected on the jetty; a girl from the Nature Conservancy Camp invited us ashore for a cup of tea, but first a sergeant took Frank to the Commandant. 'Are you Mr Dye?' barked the Captain. 'I have to report your arrival to the CO of the Army on Benbecula.' He then told Frank that a couple of canoeists had landed on the island the previous week without even water or a compass. To avoid the place becoming a rendezvous for cranks and fools, said the Captain, he was considering putting us out to sea and then charging us with a sea–air rescue. However, having been introduced to *Wanderer* and shown her arrangements, he became happier and friendlier. The Army had plenty of hot water, and we were given mugs of tea, invited to lunch in the army mess, and allowed to hang most of our clothing in their drying room. We then started to explore the island, walking through the old cemetery, a melancholy and sad place, fringed with patches of wild irises – the last resting place of the dead of a departed community. A sudden downpour put a temporary stop to our exploratory tour, and we took shelter in an old blackhouse cottage next to the cemetery.

During our two-day stay on the island we were invited to parties held by the Army (their fresh bread slabs and fresh crabs long lingered in our gastronomic memories), and by the National Trust students visiting the island to help repair the village houses. We had long and interesting conversations with a visiting vet who was engaged in a study of why the Soay sheep seem to have a cycle of deaths every few years. He told us of bygone days when the St Kildans used to visit Boreray from St Kilda on fowling expeditions and to tend the sheep pastured there. Sometimes the men would stay there a few days or longer, living in the old underground houses. They had three signals to keep them in touch with main island: patches of turf would be upturned on the hillside facing Hirta – if the upturned turf was to the left of a certain spot, it meant that the party was running short of food and water and needed a boat to visit with supplies; a patch to the right meant that one of the party had been injured or taken ill; a very large patch signified a death.

Waiting for the evening forecast at Pabbay, Outer Hebrides, en route for St Kilda; Benbecula is in the distance. Note the roller reefing on *Wanderer*'s mainsail

An interior view of the dinghy, showing the lashed oars, drum, warp and anchor

(*Above and below*) The cook on duty, busy with the preparation of food. Note the gimballed stove and insulated mugs

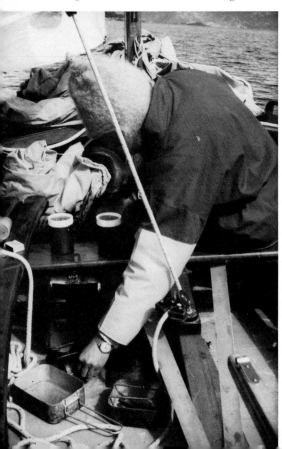

A visiting minister of the Islands was present on St Kilda during our stay, and we attended his service and Holy Communion. On our last day there we scrambled up the ridge of Conachair, and lay breathless on the grassy mountain top to drink our fill of a wonderful panoramic view of the island ranges. The Outer Hebrides were visible, nearly fifty miles away, as were the tips of the Flannan Isles just beyond the horizon to the east. To our north, four miles away, was Boreray, a lump of bare mountain rock rearing out of the water, on whose sheer cliffs gannets and fulmars return to breed each year in their thousands. Below us lay the sweep of the derelict village street, surrounded by the stone cleits, falling into the shallows of Village Bay. The white-shell sand of the bay shaded into emerald shallow water which shelved into a saucer of deep indigo depths. The sea was calm, and we wondered what kind of passage we could expect the following day. As the brilliant day shaded from blue azure into a veil of evening luminosity, we climbed down and walked along the village street, flanked with stone houses. Some had been re-roofed or repaired by previous National Trust parties, but all were wreathed in a peculiar melancholy. I had been given a tiny Austrian candle as a wedding present and told to burn it only on special occasions: we now lit it and put it into the rafter sockets of a ruined house which had been built around the altar stone of an earlier church. We sat outside the house and in total silence absorbed the quietest and most impressive views we would be likely to see in years. We were surrounded by ruined cottages, overgrown pathways, untended fields, and a village cemetery, walked over by the Soay sheep, everything dwarfed by the raw yet regal magnificence of the island masses. We stood for a long time, looking down the village street with its long curving line of empty houses. The few with repaired roofs and walls made the others all the more desolate. There was an eloquent emptiness everywhere, and an indefinable sadness; memories of a bygone age were everywhere. Snuffing out our candle, we left the area with a great regret. We rigged *Wanderer* in silence. 'Lofty' and other newfound Army friends turned up to push us through the surf, and we repeated our thanks as we waved goodbye.

The sea was calm, we just had steerage way, and seals swam all around us. Frank headed up to Boreray and then rowed hard to get us through the passage between it and Stac-An-Armin. It was an evening of burnished golden sky, the gannets, fulmars and seagulls filling the air with a cacophony of aerial voices that sounded strangely human. We felt dwarfed in our tiny dinghy, gazing at the sheer, guano-stained rock faces, on whose ledges hundreds of birds competed for a roosting place, returning each spring to claim their special patch. Stac-An-Armin is an impressive if inhospitable hunk of rock rearing up out of the North Atlantic; 627 feet high, it is the highest stack in the British Isles.

Frank gave me a course for the Flannan Isles, and went off watch. There was an air of immense spaciousness, as I sat alone in the silent dinghy, watching the burnished rocks fade. A bright moon turned the island group into black silhouettes. We took turns to sail on two-hour watches through the night, in light winds, on a course of 50° magnetic. Frank's log for 0900 hours the following morning reads: 'Decide to give Margaret breakfast in bed, for she has done well and is disheartened that we have still got St Kilda visible on our tail.' On being told to stay in bed, I turned over in my soggy sleeping bag, tucked a spare sail under my hips, and dozed blissfully, aware of clinking spoons and a boiling billy can, and dreaming of sweet tea, and hot-buttered toast. I was handed a mug of bright-green pea soup, and a greasy six-egg omelette, filled with the left-overs of the last days' picnics of cheese and corned beef. I struggled not to hurt Frank's feelings, and breakfast seemed to last for hours.

All morning the wind and the seas built up, and we seemed to reef and unreef for ever. The noon forecast warned of gales, south-westerly, veering to the north. Frank's log records:

If winds go into north we shall be on a lee shore. With Margaret's inexperience, the quicker we are ashore the better. Beginning to realise that I have got *Wanderer* into a bad position, yet earlier the approach through Harris Sound seemed more risky than the Flannan one I chose. Margaret agitating to sail; I tell her to stay below and sleep. I'm driving the boat hard as I want to have Flannan well up when she takes over.

Late that afternoon I took over the boat. Frank had reefed the main-sail to eighteen inches below hounds and had removed the jib. Pounding into wind and sea, in heavy cresting waves, we seemed to be flung down into each trough with a crash, and as we approached the Flannan Isles, the seas grew shallower and therefore more confused. Eventually we drew into the lee of Eilean Mór. Frank suggested that I go ashore to visit the lighthouse and use its toilets, since I had not solved the problems of such things whilst being flung about in an open dinghy. The 1800-hour forecast spoke of winds north-east to north, Force 6–7, so with a course set 105° to Loch Roag, Frank pressed on towards the Isle of Lewis, some fourteen miles away and visible every time we topped a wave. All that evening we dived into each trough and were flung into the next crest. We struggled between the need to identify the approaching coast before dark and keeping up too much sail, or reefing and sailing slower but staying upright. Just as the sun set, its dying rays glinted on to radio masts and Frank was able to identify Gallan Head and make a decision whether to make for it, or for Loch Roag or for Calloway. The log reads:

> Made a decision too late, as daylight has already gone. I intend to run in on a compass bearing on a mountain which should take us through the entrance to Uig Bay. Hope it's the right mountain, otherwise we finish up on this rocky lee shore as two bodies and a lump of matchwood. Margaret sails so that I can concentrate on charts. I keep a careful watch to windward, but a heavy breaking crest slid us sickeningly sideways and I only just caught the dinghy in time to prevent a broach-to and capsize.

Just before midnight, and in total darkness, *Wanderer* hurtled between rocks, which we identified only by the crash of breakers on both sides of us and slid into still water; we tacked towards lights at the top end of Uig Bay, anchored, and put up the tent to sleep, totally exhausted after the rough sail. The following morning we realised that we had dried out in Uig Bay, which was very beautiful, surrounding us with acres of empty dazzling-white sand, fringed by a ring of black mountains. On walking to the village post office to announce our arrival to the Stornoway coastguards and our families, we encountered the two remaining crofting families who were most

71

hospitable, and invited us into their homes. We found them interesting, well-read, well-travelled and generous: it was a privilege to spend time with them. The once thriving fishing village was deserted apart from these two families. The lazy-beds were overgrown, the blackhouses derelict and the fishing boats gone. As the tide flooded we left Uig Bay and sailed out to meet the sea. The wind was Force 5-6, north-west. We were beginning to feel frustrated as our holiday was running out and we needed a fair wind to make a good run and round the top end of the Hebrides. The day was spent in reefing and unreefing and tacking into rough sea. We put ashore at Calloway, salmon leaping all round us, to spend the night there. The following morning the wind had turned to the south-east, and was blowing a full gale. Frank's log reads: 'Wind off the land gusting heavily, planing very fast indeed. We reef to the third batten and remove the jib, replacing it with the genoa to hold the dinghy's head off the wind. Wonderful sailing, going some eight to nine knots in a quartering wind; boat dry, and going like an express train. The sun is sparkling on a blue sea, and the visibility is startling – we can see the whole length of the coastline, almost to the Butt of Lewis.' For hours we alternately sailed and lay in the sun across *Wanderer's* thwarts; the blue sea hissed beguilingly as we surfed over it. Forgotten were the rough grey seas and cold days behind us; it was marvellous to be warm and almost dry. That evening, the forecast told us that the wind was going to stay strong but go back into the north-west, which would give us a fast passage across the Minches the following day. As we approached the Butt of Lewis, we could see the lighthouse and the three knife-edged skerries. A tremendous swell was running in from the north and roaring on to the skerries in a mass of white rollers, with spray a hundred metres over them. Off Port of Ness we passed a fishing boat and were hailed by the fishermen who asked if we would like a fish. I said yes enthusiastically, and a large, flapping haddock was thrown into my lap. Frank came in past the breakwater, and we anchored – watched by a gathering crowd of locals. With my head bent, as I tidied up the boat, and reaction setting in, now that we had stopped sailing, I muttered to Frank, 'Haven't they anything better to do than watch us?' I was scared as I have always hated heights, and we had to climb up a vertical iron ladder attached to the wall of the harbour. My fear, however, was swiftly overcome by an invitation to tea which, as I mentioned earlier, developed into a delightful evening, with delicious fish pie and much charming and interesting company. We slept well that night, well-fed and warm in a cosy boat. Next morning while waiting for a weather forecast, we were shown locally knitted Harris sweaters, a handloom making Harris tweeds, and little models of traditional Lewis clinker boats, beautifully finished with leg-o'-mutton sails.

Leaving the shelter of the harbour we found the westerly wind was blowing hard and *Wanderer* kept trying to broach as big seas, coming up astern, threatened to roll her. Frank put back into the shelter of land, and spent some time thinking, whilst I tried to conceal my terror of crossing the Minch in this Force 6 gusting 7 straight from America. Eventually, we put out again; this time the reefed main had been packed away, and Frank had arranged that both the jib and genoa were hanked to the forestay and pulled up on the same halliard. Spare sheets connected to a jib on one side and genoa on the other as they were boomed out with the tent supports. *Wanderer* took off like a scalded cat and sailed downwind at a steady seven knots with very little rolling. Shortly afterwards the mountains of the Scottish mainland appeared, and then Lewis slipped away over the horizon behind us. Frank's log records: 'Running very fast, breaking crest all round us, but quite safe, all sail effort is concentrated at bows and no tendency to broach. Waves overtake the boat, and we plane very fast on their front faces. Steering is now exciting indeed, and we are carrying as much canvas as the dinghy can stand up to, and doing an average eight knots.'

When it was my turn to steer, I was very alarmed to feel the boat running off a wave top and then hover before picking up speed and tearing down the frothy face of the next one. Once, when there was a lull, I looked behind to see what was happening and was shocked to see great dark blue rollers towering behind and above us, curling down in a white gushing grin before breaking just behind our stern locker. Frank told me that in the days of the square riggers a canvas dodger was put up to prevent the man at the wheel taking fright on a long down-hill run and pulling the wheel over towards him. After that, I kept my face firmly fixed towards the Inner Hebrides and, while I had one hand correcting the tiller every time the boat bucked and tore into a dark trough, I kept the other hand firmly fixed over my knees in case Frank saw them shaking with fright. I did not know how to sail in these conditions. I had the instinct, but had not yet acquired the technique or experience of handling such a small boat, and I was completely unnerved. Frank wrote in his log: '1630 hours. Big heavy seas quite alarming and violent corrections of helm necessary to keep on course. Swell about twelve feet from north-north-west, and short breaking seas come from the west. Very unpleasant effect.' He remarked, however, that it was very pleasant to be able to study this beautiful coastline at leisure, because the previous times he had seen it, he had been bound for Iceland or the Faroes and wished to leave it behind as quickly as possible. He told me to work offshore, as seas would be confused and breaking heavily off Cape Wrath, and he wanted to be well clear of them.

Once the sun had set, it grew very cold and I was shivering continuously, but I refused to take Frank's advice and put on another jersey – to peel off oilskins and dress in yet another layer of damp clothing seemed just too much effort, while the thought of opening the stern locker to get more clothing, possibly to sit in a swamped dinghy overnight, was unbearable. I was glad when he took over the boat; I had lost concentration and seemed barely able to hold the boat on any sensible course. Frank's log records similar feelings of depression:

About every ten minutes a breaching wave roars by, about one foot above the level of the side decks! We keep working to the north of our course, to get further off Cape Wrath; this is not easy, as the wind and sea from the west run across the large swells from the west-north-west. As there is a difference of 25°, it is impossible to know which wave system to expect a breaking sea from, and an occasional crest catches *Wanderer* on the hop, and each time she rolls heavily we are in danger of a bad broach. Cape Wrath stays on the same bearing, and this awkward sea goes on and on, maybe we shall never round the headland – I begin to realise how it must have felt to be the *Flying Dutchman*. The swells are still increasing; the whole area is a mass of hummocks and white broken water; the tide must now be running into the wind. We can see the whole of the western coast of Scotland stretching away to the south, until the cliffs and mountains merge into the far distance.

By dusk, the seas are better but still very confused; however, those dangerous North Atlantic swells have lost most of their strength, broken up by the reefs off Cape Wrath.

We head into the first loch which we assume to be the Kyle of Durness. We cannot quite lay it – but once on course *Wanderer* tears away on genoa only, roaring down the front face of each wave, the centreboard a quarter down to prevent leeway but not deep enough to cause her to roll over as each wave catches the dinghy on the quarter. At 10.15pm there is still enough daylight left for us to round the island at the loch entrance, put up the reefed mainsail and to plane down the loch to anchor before another gale breaks.

7
ALTERNATIVE PROPULSION

When there is no wind a sailing dinghy will need oars, paddles, a tow rope, a praddle or an outboard engine.

We were once becalmed in the Danish canals en route to Aalborg. I was lying sunbathing across the thwarts of *Wanderer*, and feeling rather bored, so when I heard a large cargo barge steaming up behind us, I asked Frank if I could hitch a lift. 'He won't stop, he's a commercial vessel,' answered a half-asleep Frank, but I leapt up and made vigorous thumbing movements with a rope held up in my hand. I had quite forgotten that I was wearing nothing except my suntan. The skipper of *Sahara* looked round and immediately came up to us, eyes as large as saucers. Pink with embarrassment, I grabbed my clothes. He towed us for fifteen miles, while we washed and cleaned our teeth as we travelled. It is best to use the powered boat's tow rope, since it can be dropped off if there is any danger. The tow rope should be fed through the fairlead and led back to a secure part of the boat. We hold ours around the mast, as low as possible, but do not secure it, instead holding it so that it can be released instantly should the need arise. When under tow, the centreboard should be raised and the crew sit as far to the back of the boat as possible, and you should steer straight behind the tow rope. If the length is right, the dinghy travels easily on the wash of the power boat.

Sometimes when travelling along a narrow river or canal, Frank hops out and tows along the bank. If a long tow rope is used (the anchor warp is ideal) it can be tied around the base of the mast instead of through the bow fairlead, enabling the helmsman to steer away from the bank to avoid obstructions or shallows. Pulling with the rope around the waist is much easier than pulling from the shoulders, although the latter may be necessary to keep the rope above bushes and obstructions on the tow path.

Paddles should be secured in every cruising dinghy, but it is hard work to paddle far. A paddle is usually used for passing through moorings, manoeuvring narrow creeks, or, used over the stern, to paddle backwards.

Oars are vital equipment, and the boat should be fitted with strong rowlocks; we find galvanised ones better than plastic ones. The oars should be as long as is practicable to stow in the dinghy – for this reason, some people lash them along the outside of the hull – and they should have leathers. All gear should have at least two purposes in a cruising dinghy. Oars are of good service as a means of travelling, and they can also be used as a basic echo-sounder: depths of drying estuaries, and the firmness of the bottom can be judged with a probing oar. We have used an oar for steering when the rudder has been damaged, and oars can also be used to lash up a temporary mast, or as supports for the boat tent. Pushing off a shore can be done, without getting out of the dinghy, with an oar; if it is reversed, the blade will not be damaged.

I sometimes ask Frank if we can carry an engine. He always replies, 'Where should we put it?' Sitting in hot calms, or cold stills, I have thought often about how to solve this. Maybe it could be lashed along the centreboard, but then, where would it be put at night? If it were stowed in the stern locker, there would be no room for our tent, sleeping bag and a hundred and one other essentials. Where to stow the fuel is another problem. Frank maintains that if it is too rough to sail, it is certainly too bad to motor. In twenty years of dinghy cruising, we have borrowed an engine only twice, once to get back into a harbour before the tide turned. In both cases it was a matter of convenience, not because it was vital that we should get back. You can usually beach if time runs out, and return to sail on another day.

In many family cruising dinghies – especially if the children are taken sailing – an outboard engine is convenient. When in use, there is no problem, as it does the job, fitted securely by pad and bracket to the transom of the dinghy, and some people sail with the engine always in this position. A tin of fuel can be shock-corded in a flat stable part of the dinghy. Where to stow the engine when sailing is a problem dealt with differently in each boat and by every skipper. The following extract is taken from the *Wayfarer Owners' Manual*:

Outboard Engines . . . The Wayfarer is driven easily by an outboard engine of 3 to 5 horsepower with standard length shaft, but a tiller extension is desirable.

Some care is needed in fitting the turn-screw fastenings to the transom of a GRP boat and efficient transom pads must be used. On a wooden boat there is not this problem as the transom pads fit easily.

An outboard bracket may be used which is mounted on the transom rudder gudgeon and pintle. This form of fitting transmits less engine vibration to the hull and helmsman.

For the sake of your peace of mind and insurance cover, the outboard motor should always be attached to the dinghy by a stout line or small chain. It is quite heavy to handle if the boat is in motion owing to choppy water. Also, turn screws can come loose if not correctly tightened. If the boat tends to yaw when under power lowering the centreboard a little may help.

The aft compartment will take outboard motors suitable in power for a Wayfarer, and a stowage fitting made from a plywood panel and blocks can be secured in the aft compartment. The motor is held in position by shockcord to withstand shifting in rough sea conditions. Another handy stowage is under the port or starboard aft seat, 'locked' behind the lifting seat support and secured to a stowage fitting.

Filling the fuel tank can be quite tricky on choppy water but a proper metal can with a flexible spout will solve this problem and save spillage of the greasy petrol and oil mixture.

The fuel mixture should be carried in a metal can and not a plastic container. When using an outboard motor always have handy cotton rags for keeping everything clear from petrol mix.

For those motors with a detached starting cord make sure you have the cord with you and stow it in a safe and accessible place!

When entering unfamiliar waters do not consider it 'unseamanlike' to down sails and motor into 'port'. The professional seaman uses every aid to make entering and leaving as hazard-free as possible. If he could get out and walk to get his ship safely alongside he would do so.

Use the maker's handbook to its full advantage and always carry the recommended spares. Even on local voyages a spare plug, shear pin and prop pin are essentials.

The magnetic compass is seriously affected by the proximity of metal objects, so if you carry an outboard motor this could affect its accuracy. It should give a different reading when the motor is on board from that when it is nowhere near. Deviation of your compass can be corrected but it is little use doing this unless everything on board has its fixed and usual stowage. Do not stand over the compass with a spanner in your hand or a big tin mug! Remember also your compass points toward magnetic north and is put off a true reading of that by local variation. You can find what this is from a chart of the locality.

8
COASTAL AND RIVER

It is delightful to sail all day and, come evening, to cook a meal in some chosen spot, put up a tent, and sleep in the boat, but it is a good idea to plan the first cruise within easy reach of home, so that should everything get wet, the tent be found to leak, or there is mutiny aboard, it is easy to go home, enjoy a hot bath, and then return to the boat, refreshed and dry, to continue to cruise with experience gained. On one south coast rally the projected cruise from Emsworth to the Isle of Wight was cancelled owing to gales. Three Wayfarers instead sailed locally within Chichester Harbour; one sailor, with everything soaking wet after a stormy sail inside the harbour, returned to base to dry out and sleep at a friend's house, rejoining the Wayfarer fleet the next day. Another one – on his first rally – also got all his gear wet. Hitching his boat on to the trailer, he drove home, still wearing his soaking clothes, and the following weekend was back cruising – only this time, he had got his gear stowed in large waterproof buckets, and he had a new tent. This is the way you gain experience.

The next logical step, after spending a few nights close by home comforts, is to trail the dinghy further afield. In the UK no water is further than a few hours' travelling time away. Non-tidal waters provide plenty of planning challenges, and they should not be scorned as inferior to sea sailing – fresh-water sailing is just different. Frank and I try to keep *Wanderer* by the coast from April to Christmas. During the winter, even in January, a few hours' sail along the Norfolk Broads, a Scottish loch, Fenland rivers, gravel pits, and the upper reaches of rivers and estuaries, gives the opportunity to practise cruising techniques and try out new gear.

Whether on tidal or non-tidal water, it is sensible to use the prevailing winds. In the UK these are south-westerly, thus it is practicable to cruise north and east, and on average, you will have fair winds two days out of three. The Thames flows from west to east, and to cruise downstream with a fair wind is enjoyable, while attempting it the other way round is hard work, both for the crew and the boat.

The following account of a Thames cruise illustrates how far you can explore even with very limited time, provided you have unlimited energy. That year we could get away from business only on Sundays. We launched at our home port of Brancaster on the North Norfolk coast at Whitsun, bound for Windsor.

Wanderer spent the next weeks waiting in the mouth of Harwich harbour at Walton Ferry watching the cross-Channel traffic. One Sunday morning in early July we crossed the Harwich harbour entrance and sailed along the coast in unusually warm and calm conditions. Contentedly, we ate our chicken-leg breakfast, taking turns to sail and sunbathe on the thwarts. A total of twenty-five miles took us that evening into Burnham-on-Crouch, and we ran down the coast about a mile offshore, watching the brightly coloured cluster of dinghies around the racing buoys, and the majestic tan-sailed barges gliding by. It was a lazy day's sail, with time to stop for cups of tea at Walton-on-the-Naze and Clacton-on-Sea. That night *Wanderer* stopped at the Royal Corinthian Club at Burnham-on-Crouch. Several days passed and then she sailed out of the Crouch estuary. Again we had warm sun, but no wind. Only sixteen miles were covered that Sunday, but it was pleasant to stop on the sandbanks, to swim, stalk seals and picnic. *Wanderer* was left at Thorpe Bay Sailing Club, and once again having been helped to pull the dinghy out, we were offered cups of tea and hot baths, before we hiked back to Norfolk.

The following weekend was very special. We had the Thames charts with us, and the prospect of two whole days with *Wanderer*, a rare and appreciated luxury for me. To celebrate, I had cooked quantities of shrimps and sweet-corn flans, and brought a bottle of our favourite wine. When we left *Wanderer* we were well satisfied to have travelled thirty-eight miles. We had been lucky to get exactly the right winds and fair tides to carry us along, and there was even a strike on in the docks to cut down the water traffic for us. We left Southend in the middle of a weekend regatta early in August and tacked past the longest pier in the world. Winds were light, Force 2, but we carried the tide for five hours. We tacked across the estuary to stretch our legs in Kent, and then continued up the Thames, stopping at Canvey Island for the usual cups of tea and ice creams. The traffic began to build up steadily and we tacked repeatedly to keep out of the way of tugs and larger boats.

When the tide began to carry us back to Southend and, after tacking furiously, we had gained no ground, we tied up to a convenient post at 1700 hours and went to explore. At 2000 hours we rigged again to take advantage of two hours' daylight and the flood tide. Sailing along on a broad reach, in the growing darkness, we kept a continuous lookout behind and were often surprised by enormous ships that had silently crept up. All the warning we got was the low hum of their engines above our own gurgling wake.

The evening sail was reminiscent of a taxi ride in Piccadilly – lights everywhere: green, red and yellow; and the ordered flashing beacons of the buoys in the shallows. All too soon there was no light left and we moored at Gravesend to sleep. There were commercial boats in every direction; silhouettes of factory chimneys, cranes, and the hulls of trawlers and tugs. Almost as bad as sleeping beside a main road, I reflected, as we ate supper tied to a private buoy, close by a boat occupied by a yapping dog.

The following morning brought fair north-easterly winds and a flood tide, so we hurriedly packed the tent and sleeping bags to make use of them. The next thirty miles were exciting ones. Running at a speed of 5–6 knots we passed wharves, docks, moored vessels and huge factory façades, watching out for strong gusts coming from between the tall buildings, which in constricted waters makes one quick on the tiller. Several times, at inconvenient moments, the huge wash from a passing coaster caused us to catch a quick breath, the enormous steel sides of the huge vessels like mountains towering above our minute dinghy.

We did not find the scenery of the Thames beautiful, but it was

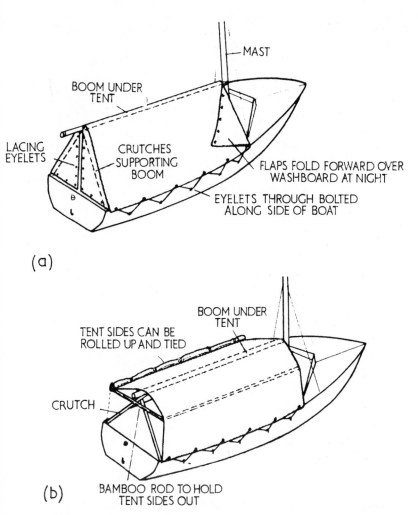

MAST

BOOM UNDER
TENT

LACING
EYELETS

CRUTCHES
SUPPORTING
BOOM

FLAPS FOLD FORWARD OVER
WASHBOARD AT NIGHT

EYELETS THROUGH BOLTED
ALONG SIDE OF BOAT

(a)

BOOM UNDER
TENT

TENT SIDES CAN BE
ROLLED UP AND TIED

CRUTCH

(b) BAMBOO ROD TO HOLD
TENT SIDES OUT

Tents: the ridge tent (a) is easy to fit and no extra equipment is needed. Velcro strips can replace the lacings at the entrance and this material is also very effective in securing the tent to the boat. Tent (b) is an improvement on the ridge tent since headroom is increased enormously; we use the whisker pole for one side support and a spar of wood for the other. The latter also serves as a portable bowsprit which, lashed to the bows in very light winds, enables us to hoist a second foresail extraordinarily memorable. The blank walls, brick chimneys, scrap heaps and dilapidated dockyards call to my mind D. H. Lawrence's poems 'Things made by Iron', and 'Whatever Man Makes', but there was little time to wax poetic (men do not like it in boats, anyhow). As we approached Gallions Reach, huge quantities of driftwood swept past us; wooden crates, wooden sleepers and planks seemed to make it possible to walk on the water. I hoped the wooden hull of *Wanderer* would not be holed.

As we came to Woolwich Reach an enormous ship pulled by four tugs swept round the corner to enter the docks. We tacked repeatedly to keep out of its way, feeling very vulnerable – the normal practice, when at sea, of staying in the shallows, leaving deep water for the big boats, did not apply here for the tugs seemed to sweep a very wide area, and to complicate matters, there was plenty of other shipping to avoid as well.

Eventually, sailing hard and energetically, we passed through the Pool of London and had seen the Millwall, East India, West India, Rotherhithe and the London Docks at close quarters. Thirsty and bad-tempered, we moored beside a main road for a lunch-time drink, and while keeping ill-disciplined Cockney youths off the dinghy's varnished decks, I reflected that the breath tests were, so far, confined to the roads. Much refreshed by pints of warm shandy, we continued our cruise. Pleasure launches passed us, and I strained my ears to listen to their guide's relayed commentary. There was so much of historic interest on either side of the river that I longed to stop and explore – but the relentless tide waits for nobody, and we had to sweep past Greenwich and a host of historic boats moored there, and other famous buildings with no more than a quick glance. I reflected with pride that we were in the centre of England's more famous past events.

We replaced our charts with a Shell Guide to London, and began to sail beneath the bridges, reading out the heights to see whether or not it was necessary to lower the mast each time. It needed teamwork and no mistakes to approach each bridge squarely, allow for the tide and to manage the tiller, mast crutches and oars accurately, while being enveloped in quantities of mainsail and wire shrouds. As it is

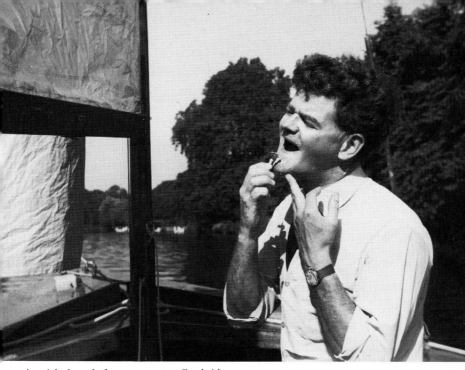

A quick shave before a concert at Cambridge

Margaret sewing a new ensign whilst approaching a Danish port

This winter visit to seals on the sandbanks of the shallow Wash well illustrates the joys of sailing in centreboard boats

Passing a well-known landmark

possible on a Wayfarer to lower the mast and both sails single-handed, thanks to an adaptation of the jib halyard, we were able to get very close to the bridge, lower everything allstanding, carry steerage way under the bridge and, once clear, push up the mast and connect the boom to the gooseneck and organise the sails once more. We only once lost the crutches overboard, and twice an oar fell into the water and so we practised our man-overboard drill. At each bridge we came to, the swearing got less, and at the end of the day we approached the manoeuvre quite casually.

Our first sight of Tower Bridge in the distance was probably the greatest thrill of all. As it is twenty-three feet above the water we had no need to do more than majestically glide beneath on a broad reach. Silently I quoted Wordsworth's 'Earth has not anything to show more fair' sonnet – forgetting it was 'Upon Westminster Bridge' – and also songs from the appropriate Gilbert and Sullivan operas. So we passed beneath Tower Bridge, London Bridge, Southwark Bridge, and Blackfriars Bridge and all the embankment splendour, and ticked them off on our Shell guide.

As we came to the Festival Hall, I suggested that the heavy work of shooting bridges and avoiding all the traffic was thirsty work, and a cup of tea at the Festival Hall would be most reviving. I half-hoped, too, that there might be a recital or orchestral concert to coincide with our visit. Instead, the dinghy was tied to Waterloo Bridge and, scrambling over the wall in outsize Wellingtons, moving clumsily in layers of clothes beneath corduroy trousers and oilskins, we waddled into the silent elegance of the entrance hall of Shell House and asked to see a friend. Minutes later we were ushered from a lift into the huge boardroom, and tea was served on the vast table with an ease suggesting that people dropped in from the river for afternoon tea with monotonous regularity.

The talk and the tea was good, but the penalty was that we lost the last hour of a fair tide. We had to manoeuvre our way under the remaining bridges – Hungerford footbridge, running alongside the railway bridge, Westminster, Lambeth, Vauxhall, Chelsea, Albert, Battersea and Wandsworth – against a strong tide. It was difficult to row fast enough to clear the bridges and get sailing again before being swept back under them. We would have liked to explore Battersea Park, but the clock was against us.

As twilight came we moored *Wanderer* in a quiet backwater kindly offered by a Thames Youth Club at Putney, and organised by great sailing friends who had driven frantically from one bridge to another in London traffic waving to attract our attention. A wonderful reunion and welcome hot meal with our friends passed all too quickly; they then drove us to Wimbledon station where we caught a train to Southend. We arrived around midnight and took a taxi from the station to our car, parked on the front. The sea was calm and the night warm, with just the merest breath of wind. The beach was in darkness and the sky beyond the sea so utterly black that it seemed almost possible to touch the velvet warm darkness, while the lights from the front were reflected in the swell. It was hard to tear ourselves away from the sea and start on the three-hour drive back to Watton.

The following Sunday we caught the early-morning tide, having slept a very uncomfortable night in the car beside Putney Bridge. The winds were light and north-westerly, and the day was spent tacking along the middle reaches of the Thames, avoiding pleasure launches and clusters of sailing dinghies on nearly every bend of the river, racing one another.

We sailed past Richmond and Kew but had no time to stop and look – a disappointment, but such is the penance of day cruising and working the tides. Late in the afternoon, we approached Hampton Court – an unspectacular building seen from the river. We were looking for a likely berth for *Wanderer* to spend the week when a voice roared across the water, from his motor launch, 'Aren't you from Norfolk?' and 'Isn't that boat *Wanderer*?' Within the hour, *Wanderer* was berthed beside him and we were enjoying a glass of wine aboard, chatting over old times in the cool of the evening, *Wanderer* safe in the Thames Motor Cruising Club.

This day's sail had been a bit disappointing and rather an anti-climax after the grimy splendour of the industrialised lower Thames. We had passed tree-lined gardens and beautiful houses with well-kept lawns running down to the water's edge – the river life seemed leisurely and untouched by the city rush – yet there had been a gaunt grandeur in the docks and cranes and warehouses we had swept past. Or maybe it was that *Wanderer* in these lush green waterways was growing homesick for the open sea and the long flat marshes of the North Norfolk coast that were her home.

On the following Sunday, after a brief walk around the superb grounds of Hampton Court (and what few rooms of the beautiful house were open to the public, as most were closed for spring-cleaning), we passed through Molesey lock. Sailing and rowing – time stood still – we ate when hungry, slept when tired and watched the racing dinghies and motor cruisers pass by, at peace with the world. The lock keepers eyed a sailing dinghy with caution, and at one lock roared at us to, 'take sails down – *now*!' – as if afraid that we intended to sail right through without the necessary chat about absent Thames licences, which we had omitted to carry with us.

The final day's sail or, strictly speaking, row – owing to the very light easterly winds of Force 1 or less – carried us from Bell Weir Lock to Windsor. In brilliant sunshine we lowered the mast for the last time at Victoria Bridge, where there were the usual goggle-eyed passers-by who watched us sail right up to the bridge before lowering the mast, waiting to roar their advice as they expected us to hit the bridge. The river was lined with trees and only a strong stern wind could have provided decent sailing, but there was plenty to see, and historical events to recall as we passed Magna Carta Isle, Runnymede and Old Windsor. I wished I had replaced the charts with a history textbook. A hot cloudless day, the beauty spots along the Thames' banks were crowded with fishermen, children paddling, courting couples and brown-bodied bikinis. Suddenly Windsor Castle appeared over the top of the trees – an impressive sight, with Windsor Great Park looking like a great green English garden.

We were going to take our sailing friends out to dinner that evening, since they had been kind enough to come to meet us at Windsor with our car and boat trailer, which we had left that morning at Hampton Court, so I rowed while Frank shaved for dinner. We then berthed *Wanderer* at the pleasure-steamer pier while we stretched our legs and explored Windsor. We were disappointed to find that the chapel attached to Windsor Castle was closed. That evening as the wind freshened we had a last sail. The sky was a brilliant pink, reflected in the water. On whatever tack we chose, we could see either Windsor Castle or Eton Chapel. Somehow, evening sails seem the most memorable, possibly because of the dying light on the water, or because of the stillness as the bird life goes to bed. The only people not happy with our sail were the fishermen on the banks.

That evening the dinghy was again put on the trailer and made ready for the long journey. We had reached the mileage limit possible in single-day cruising from Watton. Later that evening, as we left Windsor, a car driven on the wrong side of the road, hit us head on. We were travelling at only 40 mph, but both cars were wrecked. Fortunately the dinghy was not damaged too badly, although we were. I heartily recommend travelling on the waterways as infinitely more enjoyable and much safer than on the roadways.

Frank and I try to have our dinghy at Denver Sluice before the spring brings leaves back on to the trees, thus blocking off the winds and it is our tradition to sail to Easter service at Ely Cathedral, or King's College, Cambridge. One year, the pattern of easterly winds was very consistent, and one Sunday we made a run of ten miles to Ely, shooting the seven bridges en route, with hardly a pause, and arrived in time for afternoon evensong at the Cathedral. In those days, Sunday afternoon country buses ran and we left the dinghy at a friendly club just outside Ely, and returned to Denver to pick up the car. The following Sunday, meaning to sail *Wanderer* back to Denver from Ely, we only carried sailing clothes – but we were tempted by the strong easterlies to continue our broad reach along the River Ouse. Almost before we had had lunch, we reached Cambridge, another ten miles further on, and hastily tying *Wanderer* to the bank, we rushed along to evensong at King's. In our haste to get there, we had completely forgotten how we were dressed; we found ourselves being grandly escorted to the choir stalls past a congregation dressed in its Sunday-best. Horrified, I saw Frank trying to tip-toe up the nave in huge Wellington boots and oilskins which rustled loudly. I managed to grab his hat off, before we sat down, but I kept my woolly balaclava helmet on to hide my laughter.

9
LEARNING BY EXPERIENCE

With experience, you will learn to reduce your cruising gear to the essential minimum which, when packed, will be cut down to manageable proportions. It is amazing what piles of gear are collected for just a few days afloat, and I remember a particular Wayfarer rally, launching at Mylor to cruise to the Falmouth area.

Sid and Ros – great camping enthusiasts – had launched their dinghy and had disappeared with its trolley. Strolling by the beach, I was amazed to see four huge piles of plastic bags and a great pile of buckets, saucepans and even a plastic loo beside the dinghy. An hour later it was all packed in the dinghy and almost invisible. I nicknamed Sid 'the man with mostest', and challenged him to bring a portable television on their next rally. He excused his extravagances by saying he was really a big-boat cruiser at heart but he could not afford it. Generally, after the first cruise the quantity of gear is reduced with every cruise. It is great fun hunting for exactly the right equipment.

Sailing on tidal water requires simple plans to avoid such inconveniences as arriving somewhere, without food, to find it is early closing day; arriving too late to catch shops or pubs, or post offices; or having a sea of soft mud to negotiate before being able to leave the dinghy and get ashore. In areas of strong tides, such as the Thames Estuary or the Solent, tidal influences take precedence over the wind. Tides have an enormous effect on passage times and the distance covered. The average speed of a dinghy with a soldier's wind is probably 3 knots – a $1\frac{1}{2}$-knot tide will increase it to $4\frac{1}{2}$ knots or reduce it to $1\frac{1}{2}$ knots, depending on whether it is for or against you. Most nautical almanacs give a lot of information covering a twelve-month period, with tidal-flow diagrams for each hour of the tide; a tidal atlas and tide tables give even more specific information.

Wind against the tide can produce nasty conditions and a lumpy sea which make for a slow, wet, punishing sail. To stem a foul tide, it is often possible to cheat it and sail in the shallows, out of the strong tidal flow; conversely, in using a fair tide, it is often sensible to use its full strength and sail in its fastest flow. When working up an estuary or along a coast, it is often advisable to hug the weather shore, because here there will be less fetch and the seas will be less. If sailing alongside built-up areas, thickly wooded regions, or steep cliffs, one must watch for sudden gusts that swirl around or are funnelled through them and are liable to knock the boat sideways. When we have just a day to sail a passage, we always try to go downwind. It is so much more pleasant, warmer, dryer and easier to cover distances. There is, however, the danger in cruising downwind that the weather and sea can build up without one being aware of it, and turning to beat back, or reefing, may be left until too late. For the inexperienced, however, when starting day cruising, it is a good plan to head upwind and uptide. Then, should things go wrong, you can easily get back.

Before any coastal cruise, whatever the weather, the coastguards should be told, and like to know the sail number, colour of hull, number of crew, and estimated times of departure and arrival, as well as alternative plans. It is often tiresome, once the cruise is completed, to contemplate a long walk to a phone box to tell them that one is safe, but not to do so could start an unnecessary air search, and to waste the time of such a superb voluntary organisation as the Royal National Lifeboat Institution and of the coastguards is unthinkable.

The coastguards supply forms but Frank prefers not to use them (except in bad weather when it may save an unnecessary search being mounted if someone reports our boat going out and not returning). We are loners, and prefer to sail on our own decisions; if we make mistakes we prefer not to put other people's lives at risk in attempting to rescue us.

The Wayfarer Association organises Wayfarer rallies, so that newcomers to cruising can learn in company. Usually we have a good mixture of inexperienced and experienced dinghy cruisers. The comradeship in camping and sailing the same class of dinghy –

performing similarly on passage – is invaluable and an experience to be enjoyed – but not talked about.

Many cruisers do not need company and prefer solitary sailing, and certainly offshore cruises are best undertaken independently. The Wayfarer Association collects and prints all logs of Wayfarer travels, which now cover practically the whole world.

I was invited to take on the job of Honorary Cruising Secretary to the Wayfarer Association in January 1973 when we were visiting the London Boat Show. I declined enthusiastically; dinghy cruising was then for me a private pleasure, a world entered only by Frank and me – nobody followed *Wanderer W 48*. The press made out our cruises to be those of the madman or the masochist, but it was merely that we preferred to sail to quiet places and make friends with the local people when we landed. 'It is time you paid back,' commented Frank, and I suddenly realised it would be a good way of saying thank you to a wonderful dinghy and an incomparable skipper. I had no yardstick as the job had not been filled before; all I knew was that the Wayfarer Association was a lively one and that at that time there were about 5,000 dinghies sailing, most of them racing at club, national and international level whilst, no doubt, many were used for family sailing, instructional purposes and a few cruised offshore.

Several busy years later, I found my life revolving happily around Wayfarer matters – I had never enjoyed myself more. However, the pressures of a new job with unsocial hours has obliged me reluctantly to attend rallies less often, and writing this book seemed a good opportunity to recollect seven years' experiences, analyse lessons learnt and to describe how the rallies have added a new dimension to the life of our lively Wayfarer Association – now consisting of well over 7,000 dinghies, spread across the world. I have been told recently that in these years of recession, only three classes of dinghy are selling well, and one of these is the Wayfarer.

In the early days of running rallies, our sailing weekends were really practical demonstrations and communal discussions of how some of us used our Wayfarers as travelling homes. After that, I decided not always to go to the South Coast where so many Wayfarers were based, but to go where I wanted. Thus, in subsequent years, we trailed to Scotland, the Walton backwaters, Falmouth and Wales. Winter weekends naturally developed – first at Cowes National Sailing Centre and, later, on Frank's fleet of narrow boats moored in his canal marina on the Cheshire Ring. We would take our stoves, our tents and other gear and discuss well into the night how we would stow our gear, what kind of anchors to use, how we would reef and many other topics.

One gale-swept January weekend, Ian Proctor, the designer, came to visit us at Cowes National Sailing Centre to measure up our tent designs and produce leaflets for others in the Association. Dismayed by the shapeless bales of canvas draped over chairs and spread out on the floors, he decided to take them all back home, so, having cooked him a meal in a sail shed on one of our dinghy cookers we saw him back across the Solent on a hovercraft.

We now have a growing collection of slides that depict aspects of our cruising rallies. It grew out of one winter weekend when everybody was asked to bring a dozen slides of their own sailing areas and dinghy adaptations, and we now have over a hundred slides.

The price of petrol and the recession meant that many club racing weekends showed a significant drop-off of visiting sailors. Weekend cruising rallies, however, continued to draw increasing support. Because of great efforts involved in long journeys and carrying immense loads of camping equipment, the weekends developed into three days and now we have an annual week-long rally. Here, the idea is to sail on alternating days, interspersed with local exploring, picnics, beach barbecues and doing things away from the fleet. The organiser has to find good beaches, safe places to launch and leave cars and trailers, and to plan sailing venues with regard to each daily local weather forecast.

While many people enjoy the social side of rallies and sail in confidence that there is a fleet somewhere in the same area looking out for them, others think the rallies are too organised and that 'he travels farthest who travels alone'. The Association awards an annual Viking Trophy, presented by Frank, for the best log of an annual cruise. We collect all the logs which are in the care of a librarian and are on loan to Association members – so the most solitary cruising can provide a wealth of information for cruising dinghy sailors in subsequent years.

Since it is necessary that each dinghy on a rally is self-sufficient in the event of equipment failure or sudden unexpected deterioration of the weather, it was thought in the early days of rally running that an escort or safety boat should be provided on all tidal rallies. Experience showed, however, that in good weather the excellent load-carrying capacity of the Wayfarer and also her superb vice-free sea-going qualities made an attendant auxiliary boat unnecessary, which in bad weather could be of little help anyway in covering a scattered fleet. Besides, it could not follow a fleet into shallow waters, drying estuaries, and many other places that are ideal for cruising centreboard dinghies. What it could do was give psychological support and take off the crew, or tow a capsized or disabled dinghy; in fact, it was most often used for towing dinghies if the wind dropped. As many rally participants carry outboard engines, however, we no longer take an escort boat on rallies.

Outboard motors, however, also have their disadvantages. It is nice that they are available to tow a friend in calms, and to get the children home in time for their routines, but what to do with them at nights, where to stow them, and their necessary fuel, during windy sails, and how to live with them comfortably when they are not needed (about 90 per cent of cruising time) is something that calls for a compromise solution from all concerned. The majority clamp them on to their dinghy transoms, and try to forget them.

To encourage self-sufficiency, the Association has drawn up a list of basic essential gear, and those who book on a rally are asked to declare that they are satisfied with the buoyancy of their own dinghy. Wet and dry buoyancy tests are demonstrated at winter weekends.

Trailing is an essential feature of rallies. A heavily loaded Wayfarer, with cooker, food, loo, anchors and sleeping gear, presents difficulties to most man-and-wife teams, especially since some of them arrive at rallies complete with two or three children and a dog!

Never is the unspoken comradeship of rallying Wayfarers more evident than at launching and recovering times when dinghies are floated into the water in fleets of half a dozen, and the trailers and trolleys simply vanish. When evening stops are on a hard beach, a collection of carefully placed pneumatic rollers means that each dinghy is in turn rolled up the beach with about six Wayfarer crews walking beside it and replacing the rollers – a job very difficult for just two people.

Some people come to their first rally with land tents, but they soon convert to living afloat as it is far too arduous to hump all one's gear in and out of the dinghy twice a day. Also, there are many places where access to the land is simply impossible or at least hard enough to make it easier to stay with the boat.

Communication between cruising dinghies on a rally is something we often think about. On a Canadian rally I attended they carried ship-to-shore radio sets; others have devised a system of communication by flags. On the whole, one needs a system whereby, on coastal stretches, the fleet either agrees to sail independently and meet up nightly at agreed venues, or they stay together as a fleet with one experienced sailor as leader, and another as 'tail-end-Charlie'. This is fine in good weather, but we have found that in bad weather, when each dinghy demands concentrated sailing, some boats decide to reef while others do not want to stop, and so the fleet gets scattered. In any case, the local coastguards should always be told of a rally in their area and be informed of alternative routes and estimated times of arrival and given details of the boats involved. They should also always be telephoned when a rally arrives to avoid unnecessary searches being instituted.

Running rallies can be hard work but the satisfaction of shared experiences, occasional communal sailing and passing on one's experiences makes this a fast-growing sport and a most rewarding hobby and extension to one's personal sailing.

Now that I have my 14-foot Wanderer dinghy *Wanderbug*, I am enjoying single-handed sailing. When Frank decided to start a second business, it looked as though our cruising life had ended overnight. Frank's original business was a Ford Main Dealership which gave us Sundays free, but the new business was a canal hirefleet in the north-west of England which operated spring, summer and autumn, seven days a week, and dinghy cruising in November to February can be miserable even for enthusiasts like ourselves. After years of hanging about, I suddenly realised that Frank was a workaholic, seeing nothing unusual in working sixteen hours a day, seven days a week, and enjoying the challenge of organising a business, which gave him little time to miss *Wanderer* and our former pursuits. I decided that sailing single-handed was much more interesting than crewing other people, who had the distinct disadvantage of not being Frank, and I enjoyed looking after my own boat and planning my own simple trips. I found that I had a great deal more stamina and enthusiasm than I thought I had, and to hang about waiting for friends to crew, or for odd people to give me a hand launching, wasted hours; so I decided that if I had to sail single-handed certain things had to be carefully planned. The obvious things to concentrate on were starting and stopping. I found that a good low-loading trailer-trolley was an expensive necessity as I have a bad back, with missing discs, and do not find lifting heavy things practical. Slipping a boat off a trailer-trolley such as Moores of Wroxham sell, made the start quite a simple manoeuvre. The 260lb *Wanderer* floats off my trolley quite easily and, with a jockey wheel, I can walk the trolley over most hard ground, because it is well balanced. Taking the precaution of tying the dinghy to the trailer with a long line means that even a lifeboat launch is safe for the boat. I have given up worrying about recovering the boat – in general, wherever you land up, there is usually the odd passer-by who will willingly help to pull the dinghy back on to the trolley and haul it ashore, help roll it up a beach, and even offer a lift back to where the car, with the trolley and trailer, is parked. If I land somewhere after dark, I now find that I can go into a pub or a church hall, tell somebody what I need and walk back to the boat with at least one person in hot pursuit, anxious to help. It was not always so. I used to be scared stiff of living and sleeping in a boat on my own, and used to lie awake in my sleeping bag, my sailing knife on the thwarts, listening for every creak in the boat, and rustle in the reeds.

Because I was born and brought up in Norfolk, I feel a great affinity with the Norfolk Broads, as it was here that, as a student, I used to hire half-deckers and old traditional Broads cruisers and taught myself the rudiments of boat handling. With my dinghy at Hickling Staithe, I now sail all over the northern Broads, and especially enjoy nosing about the narrow, reed-lined channels, looking for unusual butterflies, listening for the rarely heard bittern, and watching the natural life teeming in these lovely areas. For a month, one summer, I used to launch at Hickling at dawn and breakfast in the early sunshine at Horsey, some three miles away. To arrive there before the hire fleets began to chug all over the area was always pleasant. Next, I decided to sail single-handed from Norfolk to Suffolk. This took three days and I covered over fifty miles, spending a night in my dinghy just before reaching Yarmouth, so that I could take the tide through Yarmouth across Breydon, and along the River Waveney to Beccles. Another trip was from Norwich, along the River Yare, across Breydon, up the River Bure to camp one night at South Walsham, one at Ranworth, and one on the Wroxham Broads. I left the dinghy at Wroxham, took a bus home, had a few days' rest, and a week later, made the return trip. I never felt lonely, finding my boat company enough – there was always so much to do and see that the hours sped by. I also found that, when sailing on my own, people talked to me very readily, and never refused to help me, if I tied up to fill my water bottle or pulled on to a soft bank to go off to shop or explore, and even offered me cups of tea, or a shower. One autumn holiday, I trailed my dinghy to Denver Sluice and sailed along the river to Ely and Cambridge. There were seven bridges to manage single-handed. Shooting bridges with Frank had become a fine art – we simply sailed the boat up to a bridge, let down the mast on the jib halyard, having remembered to unshank the lower two jib hanks, and pulled the boom off the gooseneck. The person at the helm would hold the mast on his shoulder, check that the main sail and shrouds were clear, and steer the dinghy through the bridge, which was usually my job, because it took Frank's strength to swing the mast back upright, pull up and clear the jib and mainsheet, so that we could continue sailing. This system was highly successful on our cruise on the Thames through London. But one icy-cold December day, we got it very wrong. We had spent the night at a bed-and-breakfast beside Yarmouth harbour, for it was too cold to camp out. At first light, grateful for a hot breakfast, we launched *Wanderer* into a strong tide. The temperature was near freezing and the decks of the dinghy were covered in a deep frost; we had to move carefully as it would have been all too easy to skid overboard. Looking forward to our day afloat, relaxed and well rested, we watched the approaching bridge, and laughed to see the usual row of faces popping up to watch. Seconds before we hit the bridge, I yelled at Frank to hurry as the tide was carrying us too fast. Frank's log records the embarrassing occasion:

> I had released the forestay, and carefully uncoiled the extended rope forestay on the foredeck, but I had forgotten to unhank the jib and, as I tugged at the boom to draw it off the gooseneck and begin the mast in its unhinging in the mast tabernacle, nothing moved. The mast was held firmly, snagged by the jib forestay shanks. Marg steered the dinghy straight at the bridge, and we hit it exactly on the hound band, which was fortunate, because had she tried to turn the boat, the tide would have pinned us against the bridge, and we should have rolled in and probably snapped the mast. Fortunately, because we hit the bridge square, the forestay shackle broke, the mast came down, Marg caught it on her shoulder, and the tide swept us through the bridge. The people who rushed to peer over and watch a disaster actually thought we had judged it nicely, and that we always went through bridges that way ... In complete silence, we tidied up the boat – I put a toggle in place of the forestay shackle, the mast was pulled up, and a hurried check showed that the mast had only suffered a bad bruising – and carried on sailing.

When cruising single-handed, going under bridges is much slower and more laborious. I always moor up, get the mast into the boom crutches, and row through. Quite often I play games with myself, promising myself a cup of tea, or an apple, after I have got through the next bridge. On the trip I took from Denver to Cambridge I confess that on one occasion I cheated by hitching a tow under two bridges from a passing cruiser.

I quite often reef when I cruise on my own as this means I can travel for eight or nine hours without getting too tired to think ahead. Some people I know employ roller reefing on the genoa as well as using reefing on the main. I tend to change down from the genoa to jib early on, and often sail without a jib, for in some of the Fenland rivers and East Anglian rivers, it is too narrow to tack anyway, and so only a following wind can be used. On my early summer trip to Cambridge, I saw a riverside sign saying, 'Strawberry picking starts today'. It was a hot windless day, ideal for strawberry picking and I moored my dinghy, and went to investigate. Five hours later, brown, relaxed and sunburnt, I had loaded my dinghy with countless punnets of strawberries, and rowed back to Denver to return home and make jam.

At the time of writing I plan to sail *Wanderbug* single-handed to several East Anglian music festivals. As well as my tent, cooker, sleeping bag and other cruising gear, I intend to carry a concert dress in a plastic bag. I hope to attend festivals at Aldeburgh, King's Lynn, Norwich and Cambridge, and, after the concerts, to return to my boat and sleep aboard. I have booked the concert tickets – the weather and tide cannot be booked.

Joy, an American Wayfarer friend, once asked me how she could learn to be a good crew to her husband. Unhesitatingly, I answered, 'Go out and sail by yourself, because it will teach you more than you can ever learn from books.' With this hope for myself too, I intend to continue to sail by myself, so that I can later be a better crew to Frank and *Wanderer*. It has also taught me to sort out the priorities. For example, I always wear a life-jacket when sailing single-handed, tie everything into the boat, check the rudder fitting, buoyancy compartments, and shroud fittings, not only before I launch, but while sailing as well. It is also good discipline to work out cruises for oneself. When sailing with a better sailor, most of us automatically become the crew, and do the jobs we are asked or expected to do. Being on one's own, there is only one person to blame if things go wrong, and only one pair of hands to put things right in emergencies.

10
DINGHY MOBILITY

The mobility of a dinghy makes it an unrivalled cruising base. Within a few hours from home, a different sailing water can be explored every free weekend. There is total freedom from mooring problems, and the range of sailing water is unlimited.

A well-maintained trailer is essential. The modern trailer–trolley combinations make the mobility, launching and recovery of a heavy dinghy a practical proposition for the two-person cruising team. Most people start the sailing season with a carefully overhauled dinghy. Too often the trailer is the item that is left unchecked. When Frank took two relief drivers, a carefully checked dinghy, and a good car from Norfolk to Scotland, where he was to start his cruise to Norway, it was the trailer that let them down. Fortunately, there were three mechanics and an engineer in the team, so the delay was only half a day – but they had to lash a stout tree branch to the corroded trailer to enable them to limp to a garage and carry out essential repairs, which meant using welding apparatus and searching for spare suspension units. Quite recently, Frank and I were trailing my second Wanderer dinghy home to Norfolk from its christening sail in Poole Harbour. The car had just been serviced. We had checked the tyre pressures of the trailer and dinghy lashings – but we got a puncture. 'Sod's law' ensured that it was a Sunday in February, snowing hard and the daylight fading fast, that we were on a motorway – and that we had left the spare wheel in our other car!

A good trailer gives any dinghy a longer life. More damage is done to most dinghies off the waters than on them. A flexible trailer, for instance, puts unnecessary strain on the boat during trailing. They should also be practical; a trailer high off the ground restricts the visibility of the driver, and a high launching trolley makes launching and recovery of the dinghy unnecessarily difficult. A dinghy should be secured to the trailer to prevent it slipping forward or jumping up from the trailer. We lash the rigging to the mast with adhesive tape, while the mast is tied at the mast support and also at the transom of the dinghy. The boom is secured inside the dinghy and carefully padded to prevent chafe. Some dinghies – the Gull or the Heron, for example – are designed so that all the spars can be carried inside them.

The present road regulations say that a trailer of over 2cwt unladen weight (102kg) must be fitted with brakes of the overrun type, operated through the trailer coupling. A parking brake must be incorporated in the brake system if the trailer is more than 2cwt unladen weight. A trailer and its load must not normally exceed 23ft (7m) in length, and the width of the trailer and its load must not exceed 9ft 6in (2.91m) at its widest section. Possibly new EEC regulations will make this information out of date.

Whatever the law-enforced safety regulations, if you have a well designed, low-loading trailer and launching trolley, and look after them properly, it is likely that you will have greater peace of mind when planning sails in foreign countries or new places nearer to your sailing home.

Like good seamanship, preparation when trailing makes life easier and safer. In both operations, the crew's part is important. On the road journey, the crew should be responsible for adjusting wing mirrors, aligning the car and trailer for hitching up, instructing and directing while the car and trailer are being manoeuvred in tight corners, and in directing road navigation. If possible, motorways and good dual carriageways should be chosen, even if they add to the total mileage of the journey, because these cut down the need to trail through a maze of traffic lights, towns, junctions, steep hills and narrow lanes. Braking, choosing petrol stations, and other stops, all need more care when driving with a boat.

A car which is good for trailing is one with good power, long wheelbase and short back-overhang, slightly hard suspension and the pressure of rear tyres slightly increased. Correct use of gears is more important when trailing than for normal driving, and Frank prefers

Wanderer moored in a little cove at the end of the Lleyn peninsula, North Wales. We were waiting for slack water to get through Bardsey Sound where the Tripod race is extremely dangerous to small boats

(*Below left*) A spectacular Arctic view: the Lofotens disappearing into the sunset

(*Below right*) The headwaters of the River Mawddach in Wales. We grounded in 8 inches of water and were visited by curious cows

Winter cruising in the Norfolk Brecklands at Santon; the church in the background is the second smallest in England

One of our favourite spots: the North Norfolk coast at Thornham harbour. We have stopped to pick samphire and sea holly

automatic transmission for long trailing journeys.

On many of our two-week annual summer holidays, we trail to our chosen launch, with two friends who drive our car and trailer back home for us, and we have all enjoyed good friendships, travelling through new countryside and meeting new adventures. At the end of our two-weeks' sailing, we have to return to work, and have the dinghy transported back by ship, British Rail or some other means. One year we found a rather unusual means of transport.

Our 1966 annual fortnight was one that Frank had planned for years. (He always said that the earlier cruises − before I had met him, when he sailed *Wanderer* to Iceland and Norway, were really to gain experience to sail through the Pentland Firth.) The aim was to explore the Orkneys and Shetlands. The Orkneys are made up of sixty-seven islands, twenty-nine of which are inhabited; while the Shetland Islands, forty-eight miles further north, consist of a hundred islands, twenty-three of them inhabited. Having read the Admiralty Pilots' description of the Pentland Firth and knowing that this stretch of water, separating the mainland from our destination, was the most dangerous around the British Isles, I was inclined to persuade Frank to choose somewhere warmer and easier to explore. However, I remembered that, when we had got married the year before, I had not asked him to stop his dinghy cruises as his family had hoped, but merely that I should not be left behind. Frank never broke promises, so I told myself that *Wanderer* was tougher than I, and that anyhow, we were both in a rut and needed a change. So, at 2100 hours on 12 August, we were off, Frank having cleared the office work only five minutes before.

Seven-hundred miles of fast driving, with three drivers, brought us up to the north-eastern side of Scotland, and the dinghy was rigged on the sands at John O'Groats the following evening. The next morning, after a welcome night's sleep in the local hotel, as Frank was waving goodbye to our friends Norman Meakins and John Galloway, who were returning to Norfolk with the car and trailer, I was firmly put in my place by a local fisherman who was preparing his pots for the day's work. Hearing Frank clumping down the sand dunes to join me, I pushed the dinghy deeper into the water, and prepared to swing her out seawards so that he could jump in and we could sail away. 'Don't you do that, lassie,' cried the fisherman in alarm, grabbing *Wanderer* and pulling her from my hands. He manoeuvred her carefully, and held her while Frank and I, clumsy in our heavy and bulky cruising clothes, heaved ourselves aboard. We thanked him and waved our goodbyes to the non-communicative fisherman. That night, bad weather having forced us to abandon our sail, we returned to the shore. There we found that the fisherman had abandoned his plans to work that day because he had seen a woman on his way to work. Being superstitious, a woman was to him a symbol of the devil, and would have caused disaster had he put to sea. We also learnt that, when launching a boat, you should never turn its back to the sun for fear of displeasing the gods — which was why he had grabbed *Wanderer* as I was pushing her into the water, because I was turning her head to wind by pulling the transom away from the sun's position.

After sailing through the Pentland Firth at exactly the right stage of the tide to avoid the violent eddies, we landed at Kirkwall, and to avoid sailing around the coast in atrocious weather, we decided to take a short cut across the island. The local sailing club were simply marvellous and rallied to our aid with enthusiasm and aplomb. They arrived at Kirkwall Harbour just as we were cooking our tinned supper. It was blowing a half-gale, and the spindrift blew straight into our faces, making breathing and talking difficult. They brought a furniture van down to the shore to carry the boat across, but then we discovered that *Wanderer* was too big to fit inside. So various people scouted around and found a very ancient trailer, which they 'borrowed'. The tyres were flat, so a pump was discovered; the suspension units were unserviceable, so somebody got a milk bottle, knocked at a nearby house, and borrowed some oil. After an hour of much labour we trailed *Wanderer* at 2mph across the mainland, and launched on the other side of the island. We took our new friends for a sail as a means of expressing our gratitude, waited for another gale to blow itself out by spending the day exploring the fascinating subterranean village of Skara Brae, dating from 2,000 BC, and then sailed on for Fair Isle, but got caught in a gale twelve miles off it, and our rudder broke. We lay to a drogue all night, then sailed on using an oar as makeshift rudder. The weather continued its pattern of gales and local fishermen told us that the 'Roost' is a bad sea area, much worse than the Pentland Firth, so we decided not to attempt to sail from Fair Isle to Shetland. We were surprised at dawn the following morning to find that every man on Fair Isle had turned up to help us load *Wanderer* as deck cargo aboard the *Good Shepherd* – their island mail boat. We were deposited on the pier at Sumburgh Head. Two days later, the gales died down and a wind from the south-east saw us on our way to Mousa Island. For two more days we had fair wind and sailed northwards along the east side of the Shetland Islands. The warmth and friendliness of the crofting people of these islands has to be experienced to be believed. The wind veered north on the last day of our holiday, and so we had a fast run back to Lerwick. We were back in Norfolk two days later, *Wanderer* coming with us by steamer to Aberdeen and rail to Norfolk.

One mini-cruise the following year was completely unplanned. It was Whitsun. Normally our trips are planned with meticulous care. This one turned out rather differently. We were invited to a wedding at Hull. Since Bill was Frank's crew of earlier years, we decided that he would like to see *Wanderer* as he came out of church. So we trailed the dinghy with us, and parked it beside the church, intending to see the couple married, launch into the Humber and sail home to Brancaster, returning the following Sunday to collect, car, trailer and wedding clothes. After the ceremony, the forecast was for a south-easterly wind, Force 5 and the weather was foul. The Humber looked most uninviting, and I was tired, for we had worked a six-day, ninety-hour week for months, so I said, 'No marathons'. We continued to trail northwards, looking for fair-wind sailing. After inspecting a variety of beaches and slips, we borrowed some charts from an obliging coastguard, and rigged *Wanderer* on the beach at Filey. We stood for an hour, watching with admiration as the local cobles were launched into a large swell with the aid of a tractor, then we too pushed out into the surf. With bated breath, we waited for a calm patch and then headed the dinghy out into it, hoping that a rogue wave would not roll us over, or break wrong and fill the boat with water. Frank swung the dinghy round to avoid a wave breaking badly, and minutes later turned again, then we drove through the breakers and into smooth water. We took turns to sail while the other stretched out across the thwarts, enjoying the pleasures of an empty sea, and the Yorkshire coastline. Our isolation was all the more enjoyable because we knew the Whitsun crowds were making the coast a nose-to-tail crawl. We arrived at Scarborough Harbour later that day, and I saw a poster advertising the Max Jaffa trio. So we hastily pulled the boat ashore, and departed for an evening at the Spa Theatre. Turning to smile my pleasure to Frank during the performance, I laughed out loud to see him sitting in the front row, splendidly attired in a fisherman jersey and Wellingtons, next to a plump, well-painted lady, carefully dressed in pearls, silk dress and fur coat.

Later that night, cosily tucked in our sleeping bags, we fell asleep with the waves lapping the harbour wall. The next day, after a damp walk to explore the castle high above Scarborough cliffs, we sailed on up the coast as far as time permitted. Over the bar at Whitby, we had moments of excitement, then we sailed up the river. Leaving our dinghy on the town slipway on a rising tide, we walked into the town, caught a bus to Scarborough, then to Filey, and within an hour, we had the car and trailer back at Whitby. The tide had obligingly lifted *Wanderer* up the slip, and we lashed her to the trailer, ready for her drive, 200 miles south. We felt that *Wanderer* was in much greater danger on the overnight drive home through the Whitsun traffic jams than she had ever been at sea. The following morning she was back in the field, Frank was in the office and I posted the chart back to the coastguard.

While a trailer's rollers, wheel bearings and brakes need attention and lubrication with oil or grease, and the salt water rinsed off, the trolley wheels usually have nylon bushes, so it does not matter if it is immersed in salt water. Large wheels and wide tyres ensure that the trolley does not get bogged down in soft ground, and the boat should be launched stern first into the water. It is usually fairly easy to float the dinghy off it. Gentle slopes and firm sand or good slipways make the job much easier. It is wise to walk around the area before launching from it to check that it is firm, that there are no half-buried anchors in the way, or anything else that might hole the boat.

One Sunday we had a most enjoyable sail across The Wash and completed it by sailing into the Fens up the River Nene. By the time we landed it was night and very dark; the tide was roaring out and there was no way in which two people could have pulled the boat across the mud and up the river bank. As was our custom Frank backed the car to the edge of the firm bank and threw me a towrope to attach to the dinghy. I kicked about in the dark, checking with a torch that there was nothing in the way. Slowly Frank pulled the dinghy clear with the car, and we had a meal, tied down the dinghy, stowed the gear and towed home at midnight. During the week I washed out the boat, and got ready for the following Sunday's sail. As we launched, water flooded into the dinghy. We thought that the self-bailers had been left down, but, taking up the floorboards, we found, to our horror, a large hole in the hull of the boat. A submerged stake the previous Sunday night had been responsible.

Recovering a cruising dinghy can be more difficult than launching it. The thing to beware of is soft mud. We now always check with an oar. Once I jumped out of the dinghy, intending to wade ashore. 'Wait,' warned Frank, as he always did, but I was desperate to spend a penny. The mud looked firm, so I jumped, and immediately found myself knee-deep in thick clinging mire. 'Don't come back in the boat,' said Frank, laughing at my predicament. 'Don't fall down,' he said with more concern, as it became evident I was in trouble. I lost a boot, nearly overbalanced, and could not pull my legs out of the sucking mire. Eventually Frank threw out an oar, and I walked along that. One always thinks that drowning as the tide comes in over mud is something that only happens to other people. By the time I got back aboard I was exhausted.

Some people weld docking arms on to their trolley, so that their dinghy can be floated on to the trolley in the right position, while others have winches fitted to the trailer. We have an eyebolt through-bolted low down on the bows of *Wanderer*. Using a three-part block and pulley, tied to a convenient tree, we have occasionally hauled *Wanderer* up a steep bank.

Inflatable rollers, placed underneath a dinghy to roll it up a beach, or to launch it, are very convenient. It is important to get the roller straight under the dinghy, and to do this easily you need a team of three. Frank and I once had to launch at dawn off Dover beach. There were no holiday makers around (they never refuse to give a hand), but I found two alchoholics asleep in a bus shelter and we persuaded them to help us launch across a long, steep and rather stony beach. Afterwards I brewed them tea and gave them bully-beef sandwiches, which should have been a change from their usual diet.

For many years we day-sailed up and down the coast and along rivers in a radius of 100 miles from our Norfolk home. Regularly, we would sail all day on Sundays, downwind if at all possible. At night we would come ashore and get back to car and trailer in a variety of ways — hitching, country buses or walking. You can meet a lot of interesting people doing this. We rarely used taxis, and never once failed to be back at work on Monday mornings. Walking in our huge Wellington boots was very tiring, so Frank bought a folding motor-bike. We would leave it in a hedge or sand dune where we thought we might end up, or sometimes we would take it with us in the dinghy, and use it to travel back to fetch the car and trailer. Two bulky people dressed in oilskins and boots, perched on a tiny motor-bike was a sight people did not forget.

Leaving the dinghy and returning to it later has made us many friends, but rarely we have come across boat thieves. The insurance companies tell us that nowadays a house in Britain is burgled every few minutes. Having one's boat nearly burgled is no laughing matter either, especially if one is living aboard at the time!

Frank and I were sailing along the south-west coast of Britain in *Wanderer* when business matters called my husband back to the Midlands. I had fallen in love with Cornwall and elected to stay behind and take a temporary job as beach waitress until he returned. 'Get a bed in the local hotel,' he called as he drove off. The hotel was full of happy summer tourists, so I returned to the quiet beach at Rock. Our tent was already over the dinghy, and I was tired, having served trays of tea all day in the beach café. The moon over the beach shone whitely on the sand, reflecting off the varnished dinghy masts. Rows of dinghies were pulled above the high-water line, lying drunkenly on their sandy beds; the sea purred over Doom Bar as I crept into my sleeping bag, a sandy ball of contentment, and fell into a deep sleep.

Much later I woke up: the moon shone straight through the canvas of the tent on to my face, but it wasn't that which had awoken me. A car had stopped beyond the sandy bank of the dunes. Low, deep voices could be heard as the car ignition was switched off. Fishermen, I thought. Yet I knew that the tide was out. 'Coward,' I told myself, as I reached for a torch and our knife. Normally Frank slept on the other side of the centreboard. I had never slept alone on a beach before, and I sat up, rigid in my sleeping bag, the cold air penetrating its salty warmth. Somebody was walking from dinghy to dinghy and they were coming closer. Suddenly the tent flap was torn from the transom of the dinghy. 'What the hell do you want?' I said, trying to make my voice as deep as possible, hoping that I didn't sound like a petrified woman. There was a moment of stunned silence from both sides of the tent. I heard a gasp of exhaled breath, and then footsteps pounded over the beach away from me. Somebody fell over a mooring line, picked themselves up and flew over the sand dune. Seconds later, a car purred into life.

The next morning, locals told me that there were frequently thieves in the dinghy park. 'They won't be back for a night or two,' I said.

The second time I met boat thieves was in North Norfolk. We had crept into Morston creek on the last trickle of the ebb tide. The estuary had almost dried out and the fishermen's boats, and odd pleasure craft, lay at drunken angles, their masts and hulls just blacker than the dark night. Frank was to walk back to Brancaster to collect the car and trailer, while I stayed behind to clear up the boat. We had had a good hard sail in The Wash, and after cleaning up our gear, and piling it neatly on the dinghy stern to await transfer to the car, I got the stove ready to brew up, then crept into a neighbouring fisherman's cuddy to await Frank. It was past midnight, and pulling the oilskins over my extremities, I fell asleep. A car droned along the hard beach, and I sat up expecting it to be my husband. Even in the velvet darkness, I could see that it was a Land-Rover, not our small Ford Escort. In its dimmed headlights I saw a capped, gloved, man slip from the driver's seat and go from boat to boat extracting gear. He had made three journeys back to his car before he reached *Wanderer*. One gloved hand was just about to lift our CQR anchor. 'Put that back, you thief!' I screamed from the shelter of the adjoining cabin, and put my hand on to a metal bar, just in case.

I was too enraged to be frightened. There was a long moment of silence, then a slithery shadow of a man got into the car and drove away. In the cold, salty darkness I sat and shivered in anger and reaction. Then I began to wonder if I had dreamt it.

As the first streaks of dawn lit the horizon, Frank's car loomed around the corner, followed closely by another one. 'What yer after then, mate?' said the three fishermen as they closed around Frank. We explained our nocturnal cruising habits, and they drove off cursing, having sat in a nearby pub all evening to await their boat thief, only to follow the wrong man.

In 40,000 miles of travelling, *Wanderer* has never been vandalised worse than having stones thrown at her. When we took her to the Greenwich Maritime Museum we were told by the officials there to tie the gear into our dinghy to discourage visitors taking things as a memento of their visit. So we put Henry, a mock-up man in oilskins and Wellington boots, on watch. He will keep an eye on things for us.

11
SEAMANSHIP

It is essential to appreciate the differences and basic principles of 'coastal' dinghy cruising and 'offshore' cruising. In the former, the land is 'friendly' and the sea 'dangerous', so the cautious man plans his cruising so that there is always a safe anchorage – a harbour, river, sheltering island or headland – within reach before the sea builds up, or a beach where he can pull his dinghy ashore above high-water mark and wait for the weather to moderate.

During offshore cruising the sea is 'safe' and the land is 'dangerous'. Sea room is even more important for an open boat than for a cruising yacht, as her ability to gain sea room is far more dependent on the strength of her crew. There is always the danger of getting driven ashore by an untimely gale. Most well-found yachts can claw offshore into the teeth of a gale, but the open dinghy's safety factor is considerably reduced owing to lack of ballast, danger of a capsize, an exposed open cockpit, and the greater demands made on the stamina of her crew. Even a powerful dinghy is unlikely to gain ground to windward in anything above a Force 5 – 6. My log of a trip with Rod Thompson from Scotland to Utsire illustrates how quickly the wind and seas can build up in northern latitudes.

Tea of corned beef followed by a banana, and at 1700 hours I work out a DR position, sixty miles from Utsire. There are squalls to the west, but they pass clear. I feel uneasy – the North Sea specialises in unpleasant surprises; we don't want a heavy blow close to the Norwegian coast. The 17.58 forecast was Force 7 – 8 with gale warnings for Viking, but this is a big sea area, and we may miss the worst of it. At 18.45 hours the trawler *Tistelon* passed close by and I thought she was going to run us down. All the crew were on deck with cameras; obviously they had never seen an open dinghy this far north. By this time a front is coming in; I hope we shall clear the edge of it into the lee of Utsire before the weather breaks. Wind increases to Force 6, and Rod is sailing well, obviously enjoying himself. 22.00 hours we reef main and remove jib. Half-an-hour later we reef again, down to the second batten. Wind Force 7. Seas in this deep water take longer to build up than I had expected, but they are heavy and we begin to ship water over the beam. Looking for Utsire light. As the seas build up, I conclude that it is safer to beat out to sea and ride it out to a drogue rather than continue down to an unknown coast in a gale. Rod does not agree, and takes a DF radio bearing on the lighthouse, but we only see a very occasional flash when we are on top of a wave. I gybe involuntarily, the boom striking Rod on the head, and he agrees to sail offshore to gain sea room. He is not very happy! I often wondered how I would feel if forced to go out to sea so close to shelter, but now my only feeling is one of relief to be gaining sea room which might be so desperately needed later with this gale blowing up. Close hauled due west into a Force 7 gusting 8 for one hour and then a full Force 8; we ship water. Rod throws the drogue overboard and it bites immediately. I leave the rudder down and *Wanderer* sheers about badly. We lash the cover down as soon as the mast is tied in the crutch and lay down to prevent seasickness.

Wanderer rides well in heavy seas and we turn in at 1.40 hours after bringing radio, food and bailer aft. Up three or four times during the night to check boat and shipping. *Wanderer* riding well. Very heavy seas. Twice I heard waves hissing down, over the bows, along the cover and spilling on to the rear buoyancy. By 09.00 hours next morning the seas have decreased. We tidy up the boat and start sailing in big seas (still about 10 feet) and little wind. Rod takes a radio bearing which puts us 28 miles WSW from the island. By mid-morning the sun comes out and the limp sails are banging and slatting in the light winds. Midday shipping forecast says S to SW Force 5–6. We hope this is correct as we are bored with drifting. At 16.40 hours, we row to keep warm and Rod's radio fix puts us nine miles off the lighthouse. Heavy swells are still running 8–10 feet. The 17.58 forecast says Viking gale Force 8 imminent. Just our luck! We see the vague outline of the high rocky island of Utsire at seven miles. We consult the Norwegian Coastal *Pilot*. There is a harbour at the northern end (Nordick) and another at the southern end. Heavy cloud is coming in fast from the SW and we expect the wind to come in with a bang. There is a heavy oily calm with swells still 10 feet. From 18.40 we row in fifteen-minute shifts as we want to get in, but it is impossible to row with two oars as we are rolling heavily. The clouds are dark and threatening, coming in fast, but there is not a breath of wind at sea level. As we row closer, visibility deteriorates and the island, only four miles away, disappears, so we steer by compass. At

21.30 hours there is sudden wind and very heavy rain. At 21.40 we are planing hard. The wind is SW Force 5–6. We are carrying too much sail, but we hang on to it, wanting to get in. We both sit aft and are probably doing nine knots. We need to get in quickly before the next gale breaks for we have no sea room if blown offshore.

Safety consists of never being caught close to the coast by an onshore gale with the risk of being driven ashore, and of being able to ride out a gale at sea by laying to a sea anchor or drogue. Offshore cruising may be a somewhat extreme form of enjoyment, and it can be a severe test of endurance. Sensible choice of crew, careful planning and forethought are essential. Efficiency deteriorates very rapidly in bad conditions, and it is worth while to analyse the cause and effect.

Causes: Lack of sleep
          Seasickness
          Cold, damp living conditions
          Uncertainty
          Irregular and unsuitable food
Effects: Bad judgement
          Sloppy navigation
          Irritability
          Poor quality work and inefficiency
          Danger of running down to a lee shore for shelter at all costs, in bad weather

There seems to me to be a recurring figure of 50 per cent which must be considered when planning an offshore passage. Gear failure should be allowed for at a rate of 50 per cent. If bad weather does not allow the crew and boat routine to settle down early in the cruise, operating efficiency will quickly deteriorate to 50 per cent. Water and provisions should be calculated by the same amount. Any minor injury, such as a broken finger, boil, or blood-poisoned hand will reduce manpower by 50 per cent. It may sound drastic, but I always plan every offshore cruise on this basis of 50 per cent loss factor; and if crew, stores, equipment, gear failure and means of navigation cannot be safely discounted on this basis, and the cruise still safely completed, I forget it, and start planning again. The questions I continually ask myself are – do we need all the gear we carry? Can we

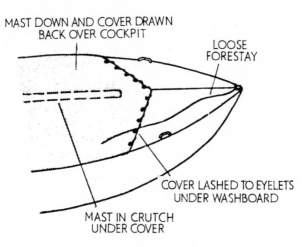

MAST DOWN AND COVER DRAWN
BACK OVER COCKPIT

LOOSE
FORESTAY

COVER LASHED TO EYELETS
UNDER WASHBOARD

MAST IN CRUTCH
UNDER COVER

Storm cover drawn over, mast down

survive a bad capsize, and how much shall we lose? What damage and breakage can we expect, and can we cover these? – and above all, what will survival conditions be like, how will the crew react to them, and will they be able to work the boat, repair it, and sail it home.

It is the ability of the cruising dinghy to lay to a drogue that makes survival in bad weather possible. With the mast lowered into a crutch, the boat will weather cock. A stout cover tied over the cockpit increases the tendency of the boat to point into the wind, and will send any water that comes over the bows back where it belongs. A parachute drogue will pull the dinghy through the breaking crests and keep her head to the seas. Sufficient line should be paid out so that the drogue is in the back of the second wave, in deeper and unbroken water. If the drogue is in the same breaking wave as the dinghy, it will pull through the broken water.

In a normal Force 7–8 gale in open water it is only the top few feet of the crest that breaks, and although this crest always looks impressive, there is little weight in it and the drogue will only be under strain whilst it passes; the rest of the time the line is slack. The drogue or sea anchor has a second purpose; it reduces drift considerably, and as few summer gales last longer than fifteen hours, drift will probably

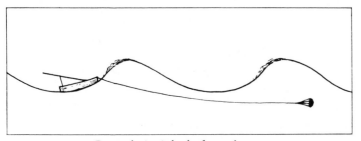

Drogue laying in back of second wave

be less than fifteen miles, an important consideration with land to leeward. I have always worked on a drift of one knot, but I think it may be considerably less.

If a heavy cross sea builds up as the wind backs or veers, the open boat could be in trouble, as inevitably some breaking seas will come in from the beam with the likelihood of a capsize. Exceptionally heavy and confused seas will occur where two wave systems coincide. There is a considerable difference between a gale Force 8 and a severe gale Force 9. As the wind increases to Force 9 'rollers' begin to develop, and waves become hollow-faced and begin to break as if on a beach. It is these walls of water that are so dangerous, because the water in them is actually moving and breaking downwards with great force. The majority of these rollers break away in the distance (ahead, astern or on the beam) and even these can be impressive and noisy, but the dangerous one is that which breaks on the bow, for it will drive the open boat under and pitchpole or capsize a small yacht.

The first Force 9 I experienced was in a 5000-ton Norwegian Express coastal liner, rounding Stadlandet at dawn. She came out of the sheltered Norwegian coast to round that massive, infamous headland. Even with her stabilisers she took a heavy pounding, and as she brought the wind on her beam to run inside the islands south of Stad, she was heeling at a steady 15°. We had just sailed *Wanderer* from Scotland to Aalesund, and from the vantage point of the passenger deck we looked at this heavy sea for some time, trying to analyse what it would be like in an open Wayfarer. Neither of us said a word; John went inside for breakfast (he was the only one) and I was violently sick over the rail. I came to the conclusion that survival in

117

a Force 9 would depend solely on how many times the boat was driven under by rollers and on the determination and toughness of the crew. Given a Force 9 that veered or backed after blowing for some time, thus putting up a heavy cross sea, the crew would not return.

My second Force 9 was with Bill Brockbank several years later about one hundred miles off the Faeroes. In eighteen hours only one roller broke aboard; all the other rollers broke away in the distance, and our other capsizes were from cross seas rolling us over from the beam.

The difficulty of identifying the coast when making an offshore passage, especially a low-lying, featureless coast, is often overlooked. I find it best to lay a course to pick up the most prominent feature, say a lighthouse, or the only cliff on a coast of sand dunes, a massive headland or cape, industrial town or maybe just an offshore lightship. It is better to lay off a course slightly to one side of the expected landfall; when the coast appears we do at least know which way to search if the landmark is not in view. When I sailed with John Buckingham in 1962 from Scotland to Aalesund, Norway, my log records how I put this into practice.

14.30 hours. Up early as I cannot sleep. I take over and John gets a radio fix which puts us ten miles to leeward of the DR position – we must have been bearing downwind slightly. John takes a second fix for a check and I work out a course of 50° for Marstein lighthouse, distance 52 miles. We can go into shelter of fjords at Slottero – I feel tempted – but it is best to sail up the coast to Marstein for the forecast is NW and we shall have true wind out at sea, whereas in the fjords the winds will head us and may be fickle. As John turns in at 16.00 hours the wind dies and I shake out reefs; it gradually increases until we are planing under full sail at change of watch at 19.00 hours. I work out reckoning: we have done $19\frac{1}{2}$ miles since DF at 14.30 hours, ie distance to go $52-19\frac{1}{2}=32\frac{1}{2}$ miles=8 hours sailing at this speed, ie should enter at Marstein 03.00 hours Thursday.

22.50 hours. First flash from Marstein just on horizon – very difficult to see.

23.00 hours. John takes over. Blowing fresh. Expect to raise Marstein light any time. How I hate picking up the coast again – the most dangerous part of a sea passage and I always worry. Write up log.

Difficult to sleep as clothes stiff with sweat and sleeping quarters smell. I hear John shake out reefs then ten minutes later put them in again. Slottero is flashing every 25 seconds – chart incorrect.

01.00 hours. John still has not been able to pick up Marstein; it should be visible by now, so he wants to do DF radio check. He does this under the head cover as the rain is bucketing down. Difficult! Meanwhile I pick up Marstein light (one flash every 10 seconds) exactly on bows and well above horizon, so it must have been hidden in the murk. At the same time it is raining like hell and Slottero is reduced to merest glimmer by storm. Blast this weather. Turn in at 01.20 and at 02.00 back on duty. Marstein now about four miles to windward close-hauled. I check chart and decide to sail up the coast past light and go in on a course of 80° magnetic which should be safe bearing clear of all rocks. We agree that the best time to pick up a coast is after dark when it is easy to identify the lights and to go in at dawn.

Years later I am still of the same opinion. It is easier, but not always possible, to pick up the coast at night when lighthouses can be seen many miles away and positively identified by their timed flash. Towns too are easily seen from many miles out, and the loom of the street lights can be seen on the horizon.

Bad weather (as on our approach to Marstein light), can make life difficult for a navigator, even one with great experience; we all tend to identify what we hope to see.

Low cloud, mist, rain squalls, and fog can suddenly reduce visibility and even make identification of very powerful main coastal lighthouses difficult. It is then that navigational aids (such as the Radio Direction Finding beacon) are so useful. For many years I have used a Brooks & Gatehouse Homer–Heron. It is simple to use, easy to operate, waterproof, the aerial and compass are light to handle and direct reading – all important features in an open boat in a seaway off a strange coast when the crew are tired, worried and possibly seasick.

When cruising I like to record in a note book the time, wind force, speed, and direction steered at each change of watch, and work out the position whenever time and weather allows. The following log of my crossing with Rod Thompson from Scotland to Bergen proved how useful this is, and how, in an emergency, it is essential to be able to refer back to these notes to make a logical decision.

Saturday 10 June Cast off at 10.30, little wind, so *Wanderer* is rowed out of harbour, filmed by BBC TV. An extra-large swell broke over the harbour wall drenching the spectators – bringing hoots of laughter from my friend John Galloway, who was driving the car and trailer back to Norfolk. Noon, and Rod takes the first watch. We shall sail three-hour watches during the day and two-hour watches at night. I make notes after our cold chicken lunch: 12.30 hours to 15.00 hours averaged $3\frac{1}{2}$ knots at 50°; 15.30 hours to 16.15 hours averaged $2\frac{1}{2}$ knots at 50°; 16.15 hours to 19.00 hours averaged $1\frac{1}{2}$ knots at 50°. Bitterly cold. During my watch from 22.00 hours to midnight two ships pass well clear. Damned cold! No darkness up here, only twilight with band of open sky to northward. Spectacular sunset with sun beneath horizon, lighting undersides of clouds blood-red and shading away to mauves and purples. Midnight forecast NE to N Force 4–5. Just what we don't want! Cold head winds again.

    Sunday 11 June 00.15 Turn in after tot of rum. Far colder below than on watch and I am unable to sleep, shivering badly and feeling sick. Rod turns in at 02.00, lays down on his face and starts snoring gently. He tells me it is far warmer this way, probably because of the layer of fat over the stomach giving better insulation. Regretfully kick him out at 03.00 to reef down. Wind Force 4–5 so we turn in three rolls. Just laying due N so tack to lay E 15°S. Rod turned in again, face down, and I clipped the spray cover over his shoulders. 04.00 a loud snap and a splash longside. The mast had gone overboard! Rod struggled to get out from under the spray dodger. The hull acts as a soundbox so it must have sounded like a bomb exploding beneath him. He told me later that he thought *Wanderer* had been holed in the bows by a baulk of timber. The dinghy looked a real shambles, mast broken at deck level, shrouds, rigging and sails trailing overboard, and the boat rolling heavily; I was so dumfounded I couldn't even swear. All caused by a cracked rigging screw (probably caused when we ran *Wanderer* under in the surf off Skegness earlier in the season). Rod comments on my 'it can't happen to me' expression. Sails were pulled in and stowed and mast pulled inboard and drill carried out as per my article on 'Emergency Repairs' I wrote for *Yachting Monthly* last September. The mast heel was sawn off three feet from the base and trimmed, and a groove cut for internal halliard. The shrouds were shortened with Bulldog wire clips. Mast restepped – very tricky with boat rolling heavily and me very seasick, and it takes both of us to control the mast until the shrouds are lashed down. Rod hoists the jib and I feel better as *Wanderer* steadies under sail. I work out the DR position:

Saturday 29.00 – 20.00 2 knots at 50°
            20.00 – 21.00 4 knots at 30°
Sunday   22.00 – 03.00 4½ knots at 15°
            03.00 tacked
            03.00 – 04.00 5 knots at E 10°S
            04.00 – 05.00 rig mast
            05.00 – 07.30 2 knots at 220°
            07.30 – 09.00 5 knots due N
            09.30 – 12.00 4 knots at 215°

Several possibilities:

1. *Norway* – 200 miles away. Still possible. Rigging almost as strong, but a little risky as heel is lashed to mast tabernacle and it might damage forward bulkhead if we lower mast in a gale.
2. *Fair Isle* – only 64 miles due N, but I only brought small-scale chart of North Sea which does not tell us which side the harbour is on.
3. *Head for Wick* – a reach of of only 60 miles. Too risky; if my DR is only a little out we may get carried into Pentland Firth.
4. *Run back to Rosehearty* – overhaul gear and pivot mast, catch up on sleep and sail home in easy stages under jury rig – or have another go if wind goes into south.
5. *Sail back to Rosehearty* – and train home. Unthinkable!

Very seasick but feel better than for some days. Wind NE Force 4. Cook breakfast, eggs poached in salt water – they were too salty, but we were so tired we finished them before realising that they were inedible!

At 09.30 after some thought we decide to head back for Rosehearty. I work out DF position and give Rod a course of 215°. Rosehearty 68 miles distance. Sun at last! A wonderful down-wind run of some 65 miles. With decrease in apparent wind, it feels warmer, and we manage to sleep in our two hours off watch. This is living! 14.30 hours. Sight land estimated at 30 miles. Kinnaird's Head right on the bows. I enjoyed extolling my navigation – Rod had already rehearsed what he was going to say if land appeared in the wrong place.

Rod identified the radar tower behind Rosehearty. Expect to be in by 10.50. Rod looking forward to personal comfort in hotel tonight. 17.30 Porpoises playing by the bows. Our course of 215° takes us straight into the harbour entrance. Not bad navigation from 70 miles out, I reflected. Everybody surprised to see us and helped to roll *Wanderer* up the beach. The local fishermen were genuinely sorry to hear of our mishap.

I wrote the following two days later when the boat had been repaired:

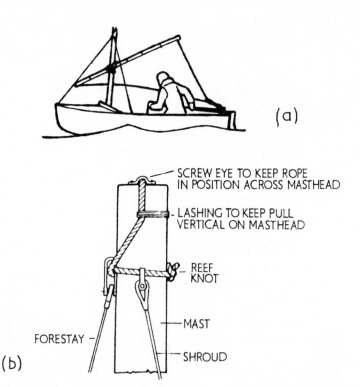

(a)

SCREW EYE TO KEEP ROPE
IN POSITION ACROSS MASTHEAD

LASHING TO KEEP PULL
VERTICAL ON MASTHEAD

REEF
KNOT

MAST

FORESTAY

SHROUD

(b)

Running repairs: a jury rig (a) from a broken mast, boom and genoa. A floorboard
may be cut up to serve as a temporary centreboard and an oar doubles-up nicely as a
tiller or rudder. In (b) are details of a jury rig, showing a lashing for forestay and
shrouds

I want to have another go at the crossing, but Rod is not so keen, and is
agitating to sail home as quickly as possible. I agree tentatively, but
intend to persuade Rod into another try. Don't know what angle to
approach this from. Foul weather with seas pounding into harbour and a
NE wind postpones our sailing, and Rod picks up a local paper. He
comes across an article refering to our cruise as a 'suicide trip', This was
just the spur needed, and with a little encouragement he was raring to go.

Deciding where to beach is a continual decision during any cruise.
To make certain of a trouble-free night when the subconscious need
not stay alert for a change of weather or wind, or other boats in close
proximity, it is good to pull the boat onto a lonely beach above high-
water mark. Most cruising open boats are too heavy to manhandle

122

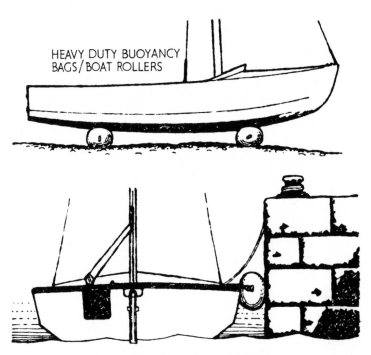

HEAVY DUTY BUOYANCY
BAGS / BOAT ROLLERS

BOAT ROLLERS USED AS FENDERS

The uses of boat rollers. It is possible to 'walk' a dinghy a considerable distance — if the beach is firm — by careful placing and balancing of boat rollers (three rollers are needed to keep the dinghy moving)

without unloading the heavier gear. Boat rollers are a great help, providing they are put in position straight, and the dinghy is not pulled over them past the point of balance.

It is useful to leave the last roller under the boat, so that an easy start is assured in the morning; but they should be tied to the boat in case it floats as one oversleeps. Rollers can deflate, and, with a heavy boat on them, cannot be blown up by mouth, so I always carry a small pneumatic dinghy pump. Using an oar as a spade we pack sand under the bilges to prevent the boat rocking. One of the most wearing things after a hard day's sail is to have to pull the boat out of the water. The racing man is alright because he returns to the same club slip where

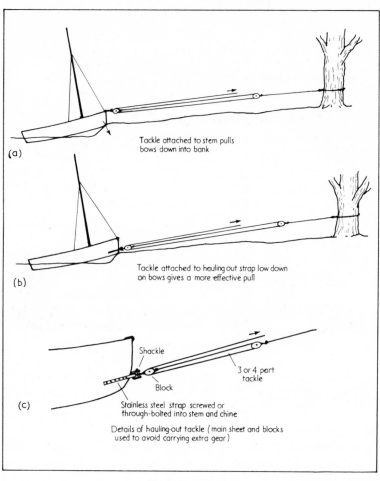

(a) Tackle attached to stem pulls bows down into bank

(b) Tackle attached to hauling out strap low down on bows gives a more effective pull

(c) Shackle
Block
3 or 4 part tackle
Stainless steel strap screwed or through-bolted into stem and chine
Details of hauling-out tackle (main sheet and blocks used to avoid carrying extra gear)

Hauling-out tackle

there is ample manpower available. The cruising man likes to sail to different places, and therefore forward planning is essential. The easiest way is to come ashore at high water so the tide will ebb away, leaving the boat ashore in the late evening, and returning to float it off next morning. Marg and I cruised the length of the lee shore of the east coast of Denmark using this principle. On all beaches there are slight channels which form shallow lagoons at high water, and we

124

often use these natural shelters to sail into and beach overnight.

It is relatively easy to get an open boat up a gradually shelving beach or concrete slip using boat rollers. On a steeper slope it is better to take a rope to a car. It is not even necessary to take the car to the boat, as it can even be controlled at a distance of 50 yards, and at least prevents the boat rolling down the slope out of control. Nylon rope should not be used for this operation owing to its elasticity. Recently I have fitted *Wanderer* with a hauling-out strap, just by the lower chine at the bows. This is excellent as it gives a good directional pull. I carry a four-part tackle which we used during a winter fenland cruise when each Sunday we pulled *Wanderer* out onto a snowy bank by attaching the pulley to some convenient tree.

One of the easiest errors if lying afloat overnight is to tie up the boat below the high-water mark. When the crew returns the mooring line is so far below the water that they cannot untie it. The first time this happened we had moored a Hornet alongside the piles of the Ouse Sailing Club at King's Lynn. We worried all night if the moorings were long enough to let the boat settle at low water, or whether she might capsize because they were too short. The following morning we struggled out of bed at 04.00 hours in order to arrive at the boat at high water to get the full benefit of the ebb into The Wash. We then had to wait for an hour until the water had dropped sufficiently to reach the mooring-line knots tied around the piles. As a result we had a frustrating sail stemming the flood tide.

Unfortunately it is possible to make the same mistake under different circumstances, and only see the similarity when it is too late. For instance, I had sailed W48 to Cowes National Sailing School to take Marg to do a spell of instructing at the Centre. After sailing up the River Medina I tied W48 to the lower part of the steps and had lunch with the centre director. On returning to the dinghy the tide had flooded; it was a moot point whether *Wanderer* would be pulled under or whether she would pull the steps out of their foundation. The weight on the line was so tremendous that it was impossible to release it. I had a quick look over my shoulder, and then surreptitiously cut the line.

One of the most important aspects of seamanship is the safety of

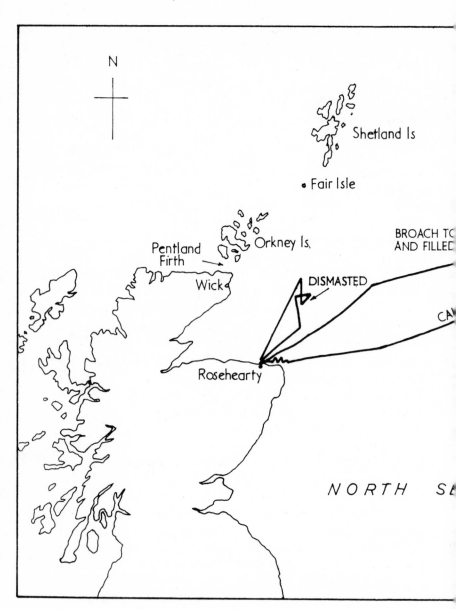

Route of the Norwegian voyage and part of the route of our Danish cruise

Sogne Fjord

N O R W A Y

Bergen

Hardanger Fjord

E. LAY TO
ROGUE

FORCE
8

FORCE
8

Utsira

The Naze
(Lindesnaes)

Limfjord *TO COPENHAGEN*

Thyboron

D E N M A R K

Hvidesand

Esbjerg

0   50   100 miles

the boat. The lives of the crew will, sooner or later, be solely dependent on the anchor holding securely, so anchoring is therefore worthy of careful study. The types of bottom are indicated on the chart and different types of anchor hold better on mud, sand, shingle, grass weed or rock. As heavy an anchor as possible should be carried with two fathoms of heavy galvanised chain shackled to its stock to help it to bite. A 5lb plough type is the minimum weight for a dinghy but a 7 or 10lb is better, with a 10lb fisherman or grapnel as a second anchor. 100 feet of anchor warp is the minimum; on *Wanderer* we carry 150 feet on a drum screwed to the side of the mast tabernacle where it is always tidy and ready for use at a moment's notice. A breaking strain of half a ton is satisfactory but we have recently replaced this with 1-ton bs plaited pre-stretched terylene to give an increased safety margin against chafe. Nylon is often recommended for anchor warp and it does have many advantages: it is immensely strong, light, flexible, rot-proof, easily handled and its great elasticity reduces snubbing which might cause the anchor to drag as the bows rise to each sea. It is excellent for towing for the same reason. However, this elasticity does have disadvantages. For example, if the boat is laying to a sea-anchor a non-stretch rope will pull her through a breaking sea safely whereas a nylon rope may stretch and allow the bows to swing and risk a capsize; if pulling up a slipway, across a beach, or onto the top of a river bank the elasticity of the rope may cause the boat to over-run. On one occasion we used our nylon anchor warp to pull *Wanderer* across soft mud to the firm bank where we could load her onto the trailer. As Margaret took up the strain with the car the nylon rope stretched, and stretched, and stretched . . .! Suddenly the suction of the mud broke and, instead of the easily controlled pull I expected, *Wanderer* accelerated violently across the wet mud like a stone from a catapult. Fortunately I was standing at the stern, knee-deep in mud, but had I been standing in front of the boat it would have been a nasty accident. I do not believe that my insurance company – excellent though it is – would have accepted my claim that I had been run over by my own boat! More seriously, any bricks or rubble in the mud would have torn out the bottom of the boat. We have now changed to pre-stretched terylene.

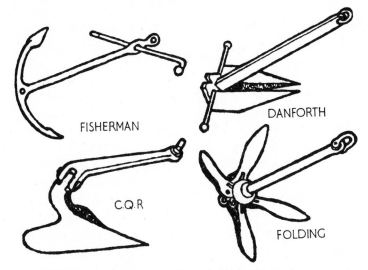

Anchors: the fisherman is good on rocky ground; the Danforth is easily stowed and has good holding capability; the CQR plough is awkward to stow but holds well; the folding anchor is easily stowed but drags rather easily.

The CQR plough and the Danforth are both excellent general-purpose anchors but the fisherman and grapnel are better on weed and rock. When the tide turns and the boat drags her anchor warp over the bottom to take up her new position downtide, there is always the possibility of the rope taking a turn round the top fluke of a fisherman or grapnel anchor and causing it to drag. When anchored in a drying estuary it is not unknown for a boat to hole herself on the exposed upper fluke of her own anchor as the tide turns. We use either a CQR or Danforth as our main anchor as they tend to bury themselves completely, and carry a grapnel for use on rocky bottoms or in case we need to lay out a second anchor to prevent swinging or the fouling of another boat.

A frequent fault when anchoring is to drop anchor, chain and warp in a lump thus creating a considerable risk of a fouled and dragging anchor. To avoid this the boat should be stopped and then the anchor, chain and rope laid out over the bottom as the boat drifts astern. Frequently we row *Wanderer* astern to make sure the anchor has bitten — a sharp tug will indicate if it has taken hold. The feel of an

129

anchor dragging over the bottom is unmistakable. If local people are about it is sensible to enquire if the bottom is good holding ground or if there are any obstructions. It may not be what it seems! We once anchored in Lerwick on sand but fortunately a local man, Tom Moncrief, told us it was deceptive and poor holding ground. I checked and found that I could pull our fully buried CQR through the sand with a finger and thumb, so we used our two anchors in tandem for security. Early in 1982 we sailed into a delightful little drying estuary completely sheltered from every direction. It was called Clam Pass, on the Gulf of Mexico with a good bottom of coarse shell sand. Our anchor dragged as the ebb reached its maximum speed at 02.00 on a pitch-black night. It was only by a flying leap ashore with a rope at the last bend that I was able to prevent *Wanderer* dragging out to sea. We were told later that on this coarse shell sand the weight of the anchor is critical – anything less than 25lb does not dig in but pulls through the surface. Had we known this we would have dug our anchor in or taken a second rope to a mangrove tree.

When cruising offshore there can be no shelter, but if coastal hopping the land is 'friendly'. The ideal anchorage is sheltered from all winds but it is often possible to find a comfortable night's sleep close under the lee of a sandbank. I have anchored under sandbanks off Yarmouth, in 'holes' in the Thames Estuary where barges used to lay, and many times in The Wash. However, it is disconcerting to find that the protecting sandbank is invisible and only marked by breakers at high water (but still effective). When sleeping in a potentially exposed anchorage, we always leave the sails on. One has an uneasy sleep with an ear cocked for a wind change, anchor dragging, swell, traffic, and a radio forecast. Mooring overnight on inland waters the considerations are different, and sleep may be lost owing to traffic, bumping the bank, or fresh-water thieves. Also seas can build up very quickly on shallow fresh water. Estuaries are not as safe for mooring in as often assumed. There may be heavy traffic and engines and people can cause noise all night; foul ground may hide stakes, anchors, and even dumped car bodies or prams. It is easy to dry out on a shelf or be surrounded by acres of uncrossable mud. It is best to anchor on the top of the tide on mud or behind a jetty at low water. However there are always unexpected situations cropping up. We once spent the night in such a safe anchorage at an Outer Hebridean island. In the morning we awoke to look over the side of the dinghy to identify an unusual smell. We found ourselves floating in a sea of offal, of distended sheep's intestines and cows' stomachs. The local butcher tipped his unwanted material over the edge of the harbour wall, to let the tide carry it out to sea. Dinghies did not normally visit the island, and he had not even suspected our presence.

A dinghy will tend to sail about her anchor as soon as sail is hoisted – unless wind and tide are in the same direction, so it is best to shorten up. It is usual to hoist mainsail if wind is ahead of beam, as the sail will be empty of wind; if the wind is on the beam or astern, the jib should be hoisted first. Pride and miscalculation can lead to unexpected results. Marg and I had spent a day in Port of Ness wanting to cross to Scotland. We made ready to leave, packed the tent, stowed the gear and had the mainsail on the boom and jib ready to hoist. We waited for the 13.55 shipping forecast before committing ourselves. Our last action was to shorten up the anchor warp, but unfortunately the anchor broke out. The locals, seeing us hoist the sails (intending to beat back), shouted 'Goodbye', 'Good luck', and 'Safe crossing'. Pride would not allow me to admit my mistake, and so we sailed unintentionally. Only when out at sea did we hear the forecast of Force 6 gusting 7, and this on a thirty-mile downwind run across the Minch which specialises in short seas and bad weather!

If a dinghy with the tent up starts to sheer about at anchor as the wind increases, it is easy to stop this by dropping a second anchor on a light line, at the extent of the swing, and letting out more warp on the main anchor so that the boat drops back and lies comfortably between the two.

Sailing at night has many advantages, especially that of not losing a fair wind and tide, and of usually calmer conditions. Life-lines should always be worn. Sector lights and lit buoys are easy to see. The disadvantages are due to loss of visibility. Squalls are invisible, as are rocks and reefs, unlit boats and buoys; and it is more difficult to calculate the wind strength.

Fog is the most feared condition to sail in. It is best for a dinghy to

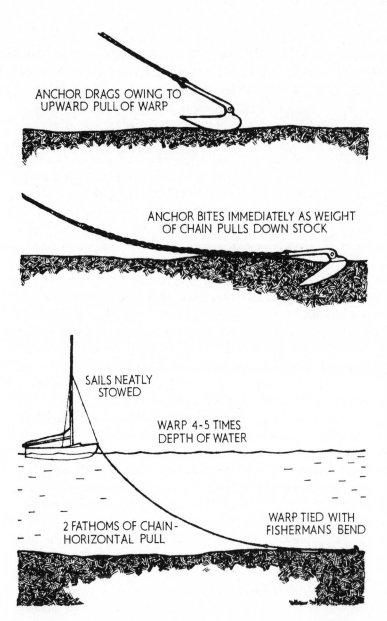

ANCHOR DRAGS OWING TO
UPWARD PULL OF WARP

ANCHOR BITES IMMEDIATELY AS WEIGHT
OF CHAIN PULLS DOWN STOCK

SAILS NEATLY
STOWED

WARP 4-5 TIMES
DEPTH OF WATER

2 FATHOMS OF CHAIN-
HORIZONTAL PULL

WARP TIED WITH
FISHERMANS BEND

The correct way to lay an anchor to ensure that it bites more quickly and gets a good hold keep to the shallows, and avoid shipping lanes at all costs. A radar reflector should be hoisted in the rigging as high as possible. Navigation is difficult, as only the departure point is known. Visibility may be better at night, but it is still possible to run into dense patches. Sound direction in fog is usually still reliable but distance is deceptive. There are many radio beacons on lighthouses or headlands, and so a bearing on a radio beacon tells when the station is 'abeam'. 'Distance off' cannot be estimated. Homing in on a beacon in fog is not recommended, and it is certainly never repeated! Many countries with sheltered busy waterways use continuous sectored lights for night navigation. Sailing along the white sector is 'safe'. If there is sudden low cloud or a rain squall and the next light does not show up, it has been known for a ship to sail right into the rocks on which the light is built. We experienced this once in a Norwegian fjord.

Crossing bars is always risky. A decked yacht can recover from being swept by a broken sea, whereas a dinghy could be swamped and capsize in the same sea. Conditions are usually most favourable at high water and all bars have an optimum period, usually two hours either side of high water. As the tide ebbs, the channel gets shallow, the water runs faster and kicks up a much heavier sea, especially if there is wind against tide.

Often it is much safer to avoid the bar altogether in these conditions, and to pull the dinghy ashore or roll it up a beach further along the coast. On exposed coasts such as North Cornwall there is little margin for error as so many of the sands are surf beaches. Our log records that we once left Boscastle on an August day at 08.00 hours.

I walk into village to telephone for forecast from St Mawgan. On returning find Marg has packed away tent, so we row out of harbour between sheer cliffs on either side. What an impressive entrance! Wind settles dead ahead Force 2. We have fair tide until 12.30 and HW at Bude is 13.30. I don't want to be later than HW at Bude as it is a surf beach and I imagine the ebb out of the estuary into the Atlantic swell could be nasty. If the wind does not get us there we can beach at Millhook at HW which will be sheltered or return to Boscastle. Wind settles into NE Force 3. We brew tea. Hazy. We are offshore about a mile and we can just pick out the four headlands (I find the contours of the Admiralty charts most useful). Visibility decreases to a mile and the two furthest headlands disappear. We stand out for twenty minutes to get help from the tide, then tack and stand in. This is an open, exposed coast, but the small islands and ridges running out into the sea help to identify it positively. The land is hazy in the mist and it gets lower and beaches appear; it must be Widemouth Bay. There is surf a long way out all along this beach. We can now see the cliffs up to the coastguard and then the flagstaff marking Bude entrance. Winds get gusty and we turn down a small reef. By this time we are close enough to see the features of Bude entrance; from the cliff a reef made up with a wall extending to a rock about 30 feet high with a beacon on top. On the far side of the estuary is sand with a long line of heavy surf. We can hear the surf; it sounds like an express train. The channel must be close under the rock with a sharp turn behind it into shelter. Whilst we hang back and watch, a big swell breaks right across the entrance; we can hear it roar, and see its foam-flecked back, dark-brown with stirred-up sand. Another roars in immediately, and Marg mutters, 'Where the hell are you taking us this time?' There is a smooth run of sea and we close haul in almost to where the swell begins breaking. A very fast tack (!) until almost touching the rock, another for 20 yards, and an even quicker one behind the rock. Looking back I can see the next line of heavy seas breaking, but we are safely inside. Marg dares not look back, and she was trembling with the tension. She had thought we would all end up matchsticks on the surf beach. A very nice spot. Relax for half-an-hour. We chat to the local boatman who said we came in just right. The shallower channel was now a seething white mass. He told us that we could be trapped in there for days, as ground swell came up quickly with no warning. The ground swell came up that evening.

When crossing bars it is essential to hold the boat true to each wave. It is best to select a suitable wave and plane all the way across the bar on it. Nothing is worse than losing the wave half way across and wallowing, with breakers coming up behind. If there is too little wind, it is far better to row over the bar because it is possible to accelerate quickly and choose which wave to come in on. If there is sufficient wind and it is astern or abeam, it is possible again to choose which wave to come in on because the boat is manouvrable. Beating over a bar is hazardous as the boat is sailing slowly and it must be luffed to ensure that it runs true to the wave position. I used to go out and practise on the bars in North Norfolk because I did not know how a dinghy would handle in such conditions.

Bernard Farrant, yachting correspondent for the *Eastern Daily Press* was to crew me racing in the Eastern Area Championships at Brancaster. He commented at the end of one race, 'What good boats the Wayfarers are', and went on to say that he had never been over the bar when there was a big sea running. So we went out to sea by the channel, came about and came in. I had picked our crossing to be impressive, but not dangerous – just about 50 yards to westward of the Wreck – for closer to Scolt Head island the seas were almost impossible for a dinghy. Even here the seas were a little risky. The first wave picked the dinghy up and we planed in rapidly. This wave was smaller than most, and it dropped us half way across the bar. The next one could not have been worse – a really large one beginning to crest 50 yards away. As it reached us it was 8 feet high and on the point of breaking; a capsize was inevitable. *Wanderer* tried to lift to it and was beginning to plane on the front face when the crest fell on her stern. We broached heavily with water pouring across the stern and into the boat, and we capsized quickly and spectacularly. I was close by the stern when I surfaced and was able to grab the dinghy. Diana (to whom I had offered a quick sail) was floating away so I grabbed her with the other hand. Suddenly a Wellington boot broke surface in front of me. I assumed Bernard was inside the boot and still under water, so I let Diana go and grabbed the boot and tried to pull Bernard to the surface. By his comment, I gathered he was the other side of the dinghy and one foot had floated underneath *Wanderer*. I recovered Diana before she drifted out of reach. Bernard hauled down the centreboard and had *Wanderer* upright immediately. We started to bail, and soon had *Wanderer* dry. Back at the club several competitors asked how we had got so wet. Bernard said we were coming ashore, and had misjudged the depth – and they believed us!

This was a most instructive sail, and I revised my ideas about crossing bars in heavy weather. I now believe it is risky and the only safe course is to row into a beach, or to lay offshore until the seas die down. It is unlikely that you will get into a beach with a dry boat if the waves are more than twice the height of the freeboard anyway.

Seamanship lies mainly in the ability of the skipper who knows his boat to judge all situations and plan accordingly but sometimes a snap decision can secure a good sail.

One winter's day, the 6.30am shipping forecast was 'West to South West, Force 7–9'. I phoned Bill Jacobs who was to sail with me, but being cautious like myself, he had already phoned the local 'Met' Office. Their version was '28–35 knots, a little South of West'; Bill commented, 'not a gentlemanly type of sailing but we aren't gentlemen – so let's go'.

With the wind in this direction there would be a slight lee from the land all the way along the Norfolk coast, and it was only this that made a passage possible in these gale conditions. However, we still planned carefully, for it is always foolish to take risks at sea where the unexpected happens so quickly.

The first question was where to launch? Heavy seas from The Wash sweeping round Gore Point would make Brancaster bar risky for a small boat. At Overy Staithe (which I always consider the most dangerous bar of all the Norfolk estuaries) the seas would be quiet, but we would be forced away from the shelter of the land to clear Bob Hall's Sand off Wells; Wells would be difficult for the channel exposes a small boat to the seas building up across Holkham Bay and breaking heavily in the shallow water of the bar; launching at Blakeney would involve a two-mile beat down the estuary against wind and tide before freeing off for the run down the coast, with the certainty of a capsize if the dinghy touched in the shallows, for she would be blown over by the wind before we had time to raise the centreboard.

So we launched at Morston into that narrow, muddy, lonely little creek winding through the marshes towards the grey tumult of the North Sea, but there was little depth of water for this was one of the smallest tides of the year. It was sheltered under the sea wall and we were tempted to hoist the genoa in order to hold the boat's head off the wind during the downwind leg, but it was fortunate that we did not for the wind returned in a vicious gale-force gust and lifted the only other dinghy being launched off its trailer into the air, and turned it over on top of its crew. It was impossible to row or sail against wind and tide in this narrow channel, and eventually we were forced to tow along the bank until the creek turned to the north and we could sail.

In the deeper water of Blakeney Pit the larger boats were pitching into a short, steep sea and snubbing restlessly at their anchors. Close-hauled now, there were sheets of spray being thrown up and blown back into the boat as our bows met each sea; the wind shrilled in the shrouds, and we were over-canvassed even with the mainsail deep-reefed, but we needed the sail area to drive her through the short breaking seas. This is always the problem of sailing to windward in heavy weather: too little sail and the boat is stopped by the seas; more canvas and she is overpowered and risks a capsize.

Without the jib to help her round, *Wanderer* refused to tack, but Bill was overcoming this by reversing the rudder as she gathered sternway so that her head fell off on to the new tack each time with certainty. This is always a tricky manoeuvre in heavy weather with the risk of a capsize if a squall catches the boat before she regains steerage way, but Bill is experienced and made no mistakes for which I was grateful as the water looked very cold indeed.

Slowly we gained ground to windward to clear the shingle tip of Blakeney Point. Once again we checked our preparations before facing the bar and the open sea – the small jib was ready for setting and would pull us ashore if we lost the mainsail because of a torn sail, broken blocks, or parted halliard; the CQR anchor was laid out on the floor boards ready for immediate use in case the mast went, for we had no wish to be blown out to sea to face the unpleasantness of a winter gale in the North Sea; the mainsail had been reefed from starboard and any further sail reduction would be done on the starboard tack thus keeping the boat close under the shelter of the land; in the event of a capsize our lifejackets would keep us afloat until we could right the boat, and our life-lines would prevent us drifting away; and we had timed our arrival at the bar for slack water to avoid the unpleasant seas which would have built up earlier with the tide flooding against the wind.

At last we cleared the end of the Point and freed off for the run down the 'Harbour', which is the deep-water channel between the sandbanks. This was spectacular sailing between two white lines of broken water; to windward there was a seething line of white water where the seas were breaking heavily on the sandbanks which protect the Harbour from the west, and only twenty yards away to starboard the waves were roaring on the beach, but between the two we were safe if nothing carried away.

On the bar conditions were better than we had expected and only one sea gave us any anxiety, but we were able to luff it in good time before it broke, and we then freed off round the green wreck buoy into one of the most exciting downhill runs I can remember.

This was wonderful sailing – long planes on the front face of each wave, surfing in a smother of foam with the bow wave rising in an enormous fan a foot above the side deck before falling back into our wake astern. Sometimes we planed for almost a quarter-mile before dropping back into the trough. From the shore it must have looked even more spectacular with the dinghy almost invisible for most of the time. The Wayfarer always feels a thoroughbred (from the drawing board of that master designer, Ian Proctor) and it is in such conditions that she shows her breeding – once again I was reminded of the exhilaration of the fox-hunting field and I remembered the thrill of the chase, the wind blowing through my hair, the mad gallop of a lively mount under me, pulling excitedly but still responsive to every movement of my hand and body, and the need to watch constantly for the hidden danger.

Looking back the shallows of Blakeney bar were a confused mass of breaking white water, throwing spray into the air and partially hiding the outline of the dark Norfolk hills behind a curtain of wind-blown spume. The tower of Blakeney church topped the low, lonely sandhills; the outline of the wide beaches were blurred by the wind-driven sand; and everywhere there was the sound of the wind whistling out of the grey sky to drive us on our way. I remembered the sight with pleasure – the restless dangerous sea, the lonely coast, the slate-grey sky and the ever present wind. It was a beautiful picture, but it needed a Constable or a Turner to paint it!

Further down the coast at Salthouse the dunes changed to a steep pebble beach, and we came on to the wind in order to turn down another reef, for the wind was still increasing. We eased the halliards and Bill tried to remove the next batten whilst I sat out to counteract his weight down to leeward. *Wanderer* was stopped, driving sideways, heeling heavily and shipping a lot of water in the gusts, and this rapidly became a test of endurance. It seemed to take hours to reef, but probably took no more than ten minutes. Each time we seemed to be succeeding the wind tore the flogging sail out of our cold, numbed hands and the wind hammered us constantly as we struggled. At last it was done; we turned down another three rolls in the mainsail and raced away again for Cromer.

Soon the coast altered again as we reached the low hills of Weybourne and Sheringham, and we talked of our last sail along this coast some twelve months before. At that time we had had a long hard thrash into a Force 6 and had averaged $1\frac{1}{2}$ knots to windward compared to our present 8 knots downwind! Over a thermos lunch, Bill pointed out the old Sheringham lifeboat shed where the original pulling-sailing lifeboat is still preserved. It seems incredible that it is only some sixty years since lifeboatmen were facing the winter gales in open, unpowered lifeboats, and I promised myself a visit as soon as possible.

All too soon the mound of Beeston Hill was abeam, and a sudden swell began to run into the coast from the north-west. These were obviously generated from the storms further north and the gap in the offshore banks between Blakeney Overfalls and Sheringham shoals was allowing them to run unimpeded onto the beach. In the deeper water these swells were 8 feet high, steep although not dangerous, but increasing in height as they reached the shallows – they could make beaching at Cromer too dangerous for a small boat and we might have to run far down the coast until we could find a lee as the coast tended more southerly.

Under the high chalk cliffs beyond Sheringham, the wind was less. We soon set the jib and came up onto the plane again for the last two miles to Cromer.

Cromer should always be approached by sea for it has a character of its own and is unlike any other East Anglian town. The sea approach always gives me enormous pleasure, and as it was my spell on the tiller I sailed past the landing and then back again in order to

savour the 'olde worlde' charm of the flint buildings clinging to the
cliff wherever they can find a foothold. Unfortunately I did not see
the next squall approaching and the dinghy half filled during the
involuntary tack (the jib being taken aback). We beached safely in a
smaller run of sea and pulled *Wanderer* up the slipway to lie alongside
the fishing boats.

In the evening, walking up through the dark streets to the flint-
faced parish church, I wondered how many generations of fishermen
had trodden this same path while worrying if their boats were safely
above the high-water mark on the beach below. Coming in from the
sea always heightens one's appreciation of the land.

Another aspect of seamanship is never to be in the wrong place at
the wrong time! The following log extract shows how, off the bleak
North Cornish coast, we were once dead lucky!

Portreath harbour has a long entrance, with vertical walls of sharp-edged
slate rock. The inner basin dries out and there are strong smells of
decaying seaweed. This is a private harbour and visiting yachts are not
encouraged. We had little choice. This whole coastline is quite
inhospitable but fantastic – the beds of rocks have been distorted into
tortuous whirls, and inclines, faults, slips, and anticlines have been
hollowed out by weather and sea. We tied alongside the northern wall of
Portreath inner harbour, carefully rigging boat rollers to protect
Wanderer's hull from the sharp rocky edges. We also rigged long bow
and stern lines to allow for the rise and fall of the tide. The 17.55 radio
forecast told of storm force winds NW Force 10 gusting 12 – straight
into harbour mouth. There was also a heavy ground sea from the gales
out in the Atlantic. I walked across the bed of the inner basin; it was sand
and mud, good holding ground. I dug in our plough-type anchor as deep
as possible, just as a precaution. We rigged the tent. By 20.00 it was
blowing a full gale, the tide was flooding fast into the inner basin and
there was a ground swell. At 21.00 it was very dark and *Wanderer* was
beginning to rise and fall violently alongside the wall, with the rollers
squealing on the sharp stones. Violent gusts tore through the harbour
entrance and vicious wind eddies screamed down the cliffs. By 21.30
Marg was very unhappy about the pounding *Wanderer* was taking. The
rollers must puncture soon. At 21.40 I decided to move *Wanderer* out to
swing on her anchor. It was going to be tricky as a wind eddy could hold
us and pound us into the wall. I climbed the harbour wall ladder and

found I could hardly stand up against the strength of the wind. The rain squalls were horizontal. I led the mooring line ends back to the boat so that we could cast off from inside the tent. I led the anchor warp outside the shrouds and tent, and through the fairlead with a check rope in case it jumped out. 21.50 Wind roaring, heavy swells, pitch black at water level. I waited for a lull then Marg let go the mooring line and I pushed off violently from the wall, on top of a swell. Suddenly all hell was let loose. *Wanderer* got clear of the wall alright, but a vicious squall tore off the tent and it disappeared into the air above us. The dinghy did not round up to her anchor but tore it out of the ground, despite the fact that I had buried it very deeply, and tore off downwind. She shot down the length of the basin under the force of the tent which had tangled itself half way up the mast and was spread out by its battens, forming a square sail. Horrified I realised that we were going to die very painfully – the boat would be shattered in the far end of the basin and we would be cut to pieces by the sharp slate in the heavy swell – before we drowned. The walls were quite impossible to climb, and it was too dark to see when we were about to hit. Suddenly the mast and tent engulfed us in a mass of splintered wood and canvas, the dinghy slowed and then stopped. All went quiet except the roar of the storm 10 feet above us. We seemed to be in a tunnel. Marg managed to find a torch and shone it around her, believing I had been flung out of the boat and crushed or drowned. Incredibly *Wanderer* had sailed herself up the narrow slipway and with the force of the wind she was almost clear of the water. The mast had hit the gangway across the slip, broken the stemhead block and had fallen down as we slid up the seaweedy slip, bringing the tent square sail down with it. There was just six inches to spare either side of the boat. Incredible but true! We pulled *Wanderer* up the slip on rollers and stowed the gear by torch light as well as we were able. It was just 22.15 – we had lived a lifetime in seconds! Next day we inspected the dinghy. The mast was undamaged apart from bruising, the tent was intact, and only the tent supports and spreaders were matchwood. We were badly scared and had had enough of this Bristol Channel area with this heavy unpredictable ground swell. Hardly the place for a dinghy.

12
CANADA AND NORWAY

Our Wayfarer has enabled us to cruise several times in Norway, to Iceland, Denmark, the Inner and Outer Hebrides, the Orkneys and the Shetlands, and around much of the British coastline. The Wayfarer Association has enabled me to cruise with Wayfarer friends in the Canadian Great Lakes area, and I have also seen a little of the Greek Ionian islands, in a Wayfarer. Frank, being a self-employed businessman gets very little free time – usually just Sundays, and a fortnight away each year. Our experience of sailing areas therefore, has only been made possible because we have telescoped our travelling time by trailing, using coastal steamers, workboats and road and rail transports to get our dinghy either to or from our chosen cruising grounds. People who charter share the same versatility of sailing areas, but cruising dinghies have the bonus that we can do it in our own boats.

Apart from solving all our holiday problems, since we rarely have a day off unless it is with *Wanderer*, we also regard our sailing as therapeutic. After our head-on car crash while towing *Wanderer* home from Windsor after our trip up the Thames, we were driven to our favourite haunt, Southwold in Suffolk, after leaving hospital, both still severely shocked. Our friends pushed *Wanderer* into the water, carried us into the dinghy and took us for a sail! That Sunday morning cruise, on a calm sea off Southwold, helped us enormously. We were later able to give our thanks in the same way. Southwold Sailing Club's energetic commodore, Sid, had broken his leg, so we trailed *Wanderer* to Southwold, picked Sid up and put him in our boat; wrapped his plastered leg up in a plastic bag and took him for a sail. Later that day, his wife was extremely worried, but Sid looked a happy man.

Being a compulsive worker and conscientious businessman, Frank had nothing to do except worry during an enforced period of leisure between resigning from one business, and setting up another. So I suggested that we should cruise our Wayfarer, *Wanderer*, around Britain. It would cost us less than living at home, I reasoned, as all our money was tied up in the business project. We launched in June from Brancaster, and by July, after a long hard flog around the coast, we rounded Dodman Point, and met bad weather. To arrive in a sheltered harbour, dry out, stretch our legs and indulge in a cream tea, tempted us to rest in Falmouth overnight.

Falmouth must have been a tiny fishing village until the seventeenth century when, in 1688, it became the port from which the mail packet service sailed, and grew rapidly in prosperity and activity. We explored the castle, built by Henry VIII as protection against the French, walked through the crowded town and along the beaches packed with holiday-makers, smelled the subtropical garden plants, honeysuckle, bell-big fuchsias, camellias, primulas, rhododendrons, magnolias, roses and blue hydrangeas, then rolled *Wanderer* back into the water, and sailed away into a quiet sunset up the Percuil river. Everywhere were sailing clubs, dinghy parks, and moored yachts, yet there was still plenty of water for sailing. We sailed on and on, round one bend in the river after another, until the water ran out, and there were no more buoys, only green slopes coming down to the water's edge; curlew and heron explored the mud. On the last buoy were painted the words 'for Restin', and we used it, knowing that nobody could sail to it until the next tide brought back the water. We crept about *Wanderer*, drying and washing her floorboards, heated the evening meal, and put up the tent in silence, for fear of disturbing that greater silence all round us. Later, Frank wrote his log and some postcards, whilst I, cosy and relaxed in my sleeping bag, listened to a song recital of Grieg and Schubert by a tenor on the radio. The lantern hung in the tent from the boom, a warm light suffused through the tent. I was sailing with a fine seaman in a fine boat. I put my head out of the tent, and blinked my tears away and looked at a starry night. I was grateful to be able to absorb so much beauty. Frank and I never spoke about the atmosphere in the tent that night – but it renewed us both with hope and peace. In a commercial world, we had both been battered that year.

One summer, Frank was unable to leave his business, and cruising that year could not be planned, and I was very disappointed. But then I received an invitation to join a Canadian Wayfarer cruise. Frank deposited me at Manchester Airport one grey, windy July day, and three days later we were launching in Georgian Bay north of Lake Huron.

Georgian Bay is part of the Great Lakes system. The bay is 120 miles long and 50 miles wide. Its western side is composed of limestone and a rocky white spine which is the Bruce Peninsula, stretching from the Niagara escarpment, all the way down to Manitoulin Island. The north-east shores of Georgian Bay are composed of bleak, rocky Canadian Shield territory. The deep ravines left by the retreating glaciated fingers of ice are still vividly seen in the low-lying pink rocky coastline. There are at least fifty thousand islands in the bay's vicinity, many uninhabited. In bygone days, these glaciated waterways and huge tideless fresh-water seas were the highways for voyageurs and fur traders. Now, four centuries later, I was sailing over the same area, listening to the same wind, in the same pine trees, scrambling over the same rocks coated in moss and lichens, dwarf iris, marsh marigolds, indian paint brush and wild orchids, and experiencing the vast wildness of this Canadian landscape. As I stood, listening to the surf breaking on the windward shore, and to the plaintive whip-poor-wills and loons, I felt that four centuries of humanity had not altered this primeval landscape one iota. We sailed on, past the Cloche mountains, with the glistening quartz shining whitely between the belts of cedar and pine trees. The pine trees bent grotesquely, like old men, bowing in silent resignation to the prevailing winds. As the light winds died, we rowed into a rocky bay, tied to the trees, and laid out stern anchors. We had had a splendid sail, and it was still only 1600 hours, with a long sunny evening for exploring. We walked around, watched turtles and snakes swimming in the clear blue waters, collected blueberries, raspberries, and followed butterflies and enormous dragonflies. Treading carefully to avoid stepping on purple-fringed orchids and pink lady's slippers, we returned to the dinghies. I knew great peace; the big blue sky darkened to a velvet pall, the island waters dimmed from purest turquoise to indigo blue. We slept deeply that night in Beaverstone Bay; our camp site was in Indian Reserve No 3.

After two glorious weeks' sailing and camping amongst the uninhabited islands, it was time to return home. All four dinghies sailed into Tobermory at about midday. As we unpacked and prepared to load the Wayfarers on to the road trailers, the Canadian and American holiday-makers eyed us with interest. They were sunbathing on the decks of their sumptuous motor launches and motor sailers; dinghies were not often seen in this part of the world. Bales of gear came out of the dinghies, Joy neatly changed into shore-going clothes, and all nine of us piled into Pete's dinghy for the final cocktail hour. We were plied with questions – 'How do you manage without a cabin?' – 'What is that little boat?' – 'How do you sleep on her?' – 'Where have you been?' I think that they envied us. Bill watched one of their launches filling up; it greedily drank over forty gallons of fuel – they would not explore far into Georgian Bay on that!

Another year we appreciated in Arctic Norway, as I had done in Canada, that people are as important as natural beauty.

Ahead of us enormous mountains rose straight from the sea, their ragged peaks tipped by white fleecy clouds and a glacier covering the uplands between them. Far on the starboard bow, two fjords cut deeply into the land, and the few minute houses by the edge of the sea emphasised the vastness of this country.

We altered course a little, towards Jokelfjord where we had been told the glacier calves into the sea – the only one to do so in Europe. Out in the open there was plenty of wind and we were sailing fast on a fine reach with a reef in the mainsail, but as we entered the fjord the wind dropped and we shook out our reefs.

The mountains to port were enormous, with sheer black rock rising vertically from the water to over 2,000 feet; on the other side of the fjord there were painted houses and light green fields, but they were several miles away and close under the rocks there was a darkness and a deep feeling of gloom; the stillness was so complete that it could be felt.

As we sailed further down the fjord we noticed hundreds of gulls fishing and we got out our fishing line and spinner, thinking we were probably being optimistic as we had been told we must fish below 300 metres to catch good fish. Immediately there was a tug on the line and we reeled in a good *sai* (coalfish) which we put in the bucket for supper. Next came a really good codfish, which made the nylon line cut whitely into Frank's fingers as he pulled it in. Then two more coalfish which we threw back, as we already had enough for the next two days.

The wind was still dropping and a fisherman in a motor skiff came alongside, and seeing our British ensign, grunted a greeting and towed us to a little jetty where we tied alongside his fishing boat. He tried hard to hide his surprise that Frank had a girl crew – sailing dinghies in North Norway are very rare and female crew are unheard of! He had no English and we cannot speak Norwegian, but somehow we managed to chat about our holiday in Norway, our liking for his country and the excellent fishing. We proudly showed him our cod, but he laughed at us and suggested we throw it back, as it was too small to eat. He showed us some of the cod that he had caught, all over four feet long.

While we were talking a Lapp rowed over, dressed in the beautiful traditional red clothing and soft leather boots, but we could not understand what he was trying to sell us. I thought that it might be two cheeses, which would make excellent presents, and we walked across to his boat to inspect. Looking over the side of the boat we came face to face with two reindeer which he had just slaughtered and skinned. He grinned at our surprise and said that he could not possibly sell them for less than 100 kroner (about £6). Frank was greatly tempted, for like all game, reindeer needs hanging for at least ten days and this would just fit in nicely with our return plans, and if we left all our gear in Norway, we could just take one carcass, which could be divided up to make excellent presents, within our baggage allowance on our flight home. After some discussion we refused his offer with regret for we were not sure that the customs would pass it, even if we did call it a souvenir!

The fisherman discovered that we wanted to see the glacier and said that he would motor us up to the head of the fjord to see the ice. We set off up the fjord at a steady rate of 8 knots, with the fjord becoming narrower and darker as the mountains closed in from both sides; there was not a breath of wind, and the water was so still that the whole scene was reflected as if in a mirror, and in the far distance we could see the ice field spilling over the edge of a mountain into the valley. Round the last bend the whole of the fjord came into view – a tremendous disappointment, for we had expected an enormous cascade of ice, icebergs floating in the fjord, the 'crack' of the ice breaking and so on, but everything was completely still and the glacier apparently a mere ribbon down the side of the mountain, ending in a small beach at the head of the fjord. Our Norwegian friend changed course a little and we continued motoring for mile after mile, beginning to realise how deceptive was the distance. Half an hour later we ran on the little beach beneath the glacier and we could see the enormous size of it – what had looked, in the distance, like a little trickle of water running out from beneath the ice, was now a raging torrent pouring out of ice caves 60 feet high, the roar of the waterfall filling the whole fjord and making conversation impossible, except by shouting. The little beach was now some 300 yards wide, made up of pebbles of granite ground down by the ice into perfect spheres each the size of a pea, and studded with enormous boulders, some 20 feet in diameter, several covered with the shells of limpets, which was very surprising as they were well above high water. Our host explained that each time the glacier calves into the sea the tidal waves pick up boulders from the bottom and throw them on to the beach where they are ground down into pebbles by the tides the following winter. Beyond the beach there was another half-mile of still, green water between us and the ice and we gazed about us, awed by the magnificent scenery, the deep gloom, the intense stillness, the brilliant green of the ice towering 4,000 feet above us and the booming roar of the water, echoing from the mountains on all sides. Clouds had gathered round the crags, and were now edging down into the fjord, giving the valley an eerie and mystical touch. The gloom deepened and the clouds reached down; we looked back down the fjord to see the sun shining on the houses many miles away and realised what a lonely, frightening place it is and understood so much better the violence of the old Norse mythology.

Our fisherman friend, Mr Nilsen, noticed Frank testing the water and said that a local man had caught 200 salmon in one afternoon in the cold water at the head of the fjord. Each yuletide, he told me, he came here to cut a Christmas tree for his family, and for the first time we noticed that the lower slopes were covered with trees. He then invited us to meet his wife, and these charming and hospitable people insisted that we stay with them overnight rather than sleep in a wet boat. The next morning Mrs Nilsen pressed breakfast upon us before we left – an enormous meal of home-smoked salmon, pancakes and sweet goat's-milk cheese, and lashings of cloudberry jam. As we left she pressed into my hands an enormous bag of fresh cloudberries, and said in Norwegian, 'to be eaten with your little cod for supper tonight'.

As we sailed down the fjord towards the gale that was blowing outside, we both looked back and thought how lucky we were that chance had brought us the memorable experience of sailing into Jokelfjord.

Indeed, throughout our lives, planning the next dinghy cruise or remembering the highlights of the last one, has provided us with more satisfactions and challenges than any other occupation we have yet discovered. Only a few months before writing this final chapter we put *Wanderer* in a container and shipped her to the USA, where we spent a month sailing across Florida by canal, lake and river, then south through the Everglades National Park and around the sunny southern tip. All this while the UK was buried beneath the winter snows! We were so impressed by the beautiful sailing waters of this new (to us) continent that we made a snap decision to keep *Wanderer* there and at the time of writing we intend to return and sail to new places. The range of a cruising dinghy is endless.

APPENDIX A
Cruising Equipment Check List

Address book
Anchor chain, warp and drum
Anchors

Battens
Bedding (down sleeping bags in water-proof cases plus lilos)
Binoculars (or telescope)
Boom
Boom crutches (long and short pair)
Bosun's box
Buckets (with water-tight lids)

Camera (and films in water-proof box)
Centreboard and pivot
Charts
Clothing (spares, separately wrapped and in a large water-proof sack)
Compasses
Cutlery (one set per person and one spare)

Ensign staff
Ensigns (courtesy)

Fenders
First-aid kit
Fishing tackle
Flare packs
Floorboards
Foghorn
Food
Forecast record pad
Forestay

Grease-grun (for trailer)

Hatchcover

Insurance papers (useful for proof of boat's identity)

Kicking-strap
Knives (floating one, and one with a retractable blade)

Lantern and fuel
Lead-sounding equipment
Licences
Lifelines and life jackets
Lock paddle keys
Log-book
Long warps

Mainsheet and blocks
Mast and pivot
Mastic
Matches
Money
Mugs (we use insulated ones to feed from, as well as for drinks; food keeps hotter, spills less easily and it is easier to eat singlehanded)

Nautical Almanac
Navigational instruments

Oilskins and patching kits
Ordnance Survey maps

Paddle
Passport
Patches (of plywood)
Pilot books and relevant sailing instructions
Plimsoles
Pots and pans (billy cans, kettle; stacking pots and the non-stick

good to use)
ast two different types)

Radar reflector
Radio (RDF set is good)
Rollers (pneumatic)
Rowlocks (two sets)
Rudder

Sacks (storage of clothing, food, garbage etc)
Sails and sail-repair kit
Scoop and sponge
Spectacles and sunglasses
Sponge bag
Stove and fuel

Telescope (or binoculars)
Tent
Tidal-streams atlases
Tiller

Tin-openers
Toilet paper
Tool box
Torches and batteries

Warps
Water containers (screw tops)
Wellingtons (we wear one size too large to kick off in event of a capsize)
Whisker pole (tent support)
NB 1. Most articles should have lanyards on them.
2. Most articles should have a dual purpose in any cruising dinghy where space and weight are at a premium. For example, our whisker pole is also our tent 'side' support.

APPENDIX B

Dinghy Tents

When cruising it is often convenient to sleep in a tent erected on the dinghy itself. In this way you can dry out or remain afloat at will and be less dependent on shore facilities.

No definitive guidelines can be laid down here since there are many types of tent available. Each owner must decide whether the tent should be of natural or artificial material, whether the design shall be simple and quick to put up – and possibly cramped – or spacious and more time-consuming to erect. The decision largely depends on the size of the crew, time spent afloat, and how much one is prepared to pay for a tent. Frank and I have a tent made out of treble-proofed Egyptian cotton; this is expensive but it is waterproof and airy, it is easy to mend (and add pieces to if it should shrink) and it provides 2ft 6in sitting headroom. It is hung over the boom – which rests in a crutch sitting on the transom deck – and it takes us about thirty minutes to convert the cockpit into a cosy cabin. A rigid framework or structure for the tent is vital; it can be made of virtually any material provided it is light, non-corrosive and reliable. We use bamboo rods as side supports, fastened at one end to a cross-piece on the boom-crutch and to a shroud at the other. Furthermore, wooden supports will float in the event of a capsize and can be modified if the tent shrinks.

The tent can be attached to the boat in several ways: by shock cord led down from eyelets in the tent to hooks or trumpet cleats beneath the rubbing strake; velcro strips on the tent can be secured to velcro strips glued and pinned (with small brass nails) beneath the rubbing strake; or the tent can be fastened to a removable bolt rope around the dinghy hull. What is important to remember is that the tent must be fixed from inside the boat as it is not always possible to land and walk around the boat to check all fastenings. In an emergency the tent must be quickly and easily removable.

It is advisable to have two openings in the tent, usually one over the transom and one over the bows. They can be sealed with velcro strips, plastic or metal zips, or lacings. Velcro strips have the advantage over zips in that they cannot corrode, jam or refuse to seal. Lacings keep the tent rain- and windproof, but they may take too long to undo in an emergency. Whatever method is adopted it is important that it is reliable, quick, non-corrosive and resistant to salt water. We like a second method in case the primary one breaks away, so we have plastic zips overlaid with a flap and velcro strip.

The tent seems to make little difference to a dinghy riding at anchor, and the windage of most tents seems unimportant as the dinghy swings to wind or tide. Often it is possible to roll the dinghy above the high-water mark, and chock the dinghy level with soft sand or roller inflatables. An even easier way to sleep securely is to dry out on a nice sandy flat beach at a dusk high water; by breakfast time the tide has returned to float one off again.

INDEX